FLOWERS AND BUT
IN 3D BOBBIN LACE

30 Patterns
for the non-specialist lacemaker
who is looking for
something
pleasantly different

Dorothy K Cox

To Anne,
my gardening daughter-in-law in NSW

ACKNOWLEDGEMENTS

I have greatly valued the encouragement and help of several of the Brigantes Lacemakers in Harrogate who have acted as guinea pigs for some of my instructions; Elaine Armes has also been most helpful. My daughter Rosemary was responsible for the photographs and the cover painting. Mainly, however, it is a tolerant and ever-supportive husband who has made this project possible.

By the same author
Before Grey Rabbit
Making Lace With Little Grey Rabbit

Flowers and Butterflies in 3D Bobbin Lace

ISBN 0 9508558 2 0

D K Cox, 43 St Winifred's Road, HARROGATE, N Yorks HG2 8LW

Printed by A. R. Facer Ltd., Horsforth, Leeds.

CONTENTS

INTRODUCTION

It was at the Lace Guild Exhibition in 1978 that I first came across Joyce Willmot's 3D flowers, but several years passed before we met. Apart from lace, my main hobbies are gardening, flower arranging and flower painting, so it was inevitable that I should be entranced by yet another form of floral art, and I shall be ever grateful to Joyce for the hours of pleasure she has inspired.

In the book 'Lace Flowers And How To Make Them' all the flowers are sufficiently firm to need no extra support, but larger life-sized flowers are helped by some additional stiffening, and it is the purpose of this collection to complement Joyce Willmot's book by introducing wired petals. Most of these patterns are taken from actual flowers and although the lace does shrink slightly when the pins are removed the effect is authentic.

Many flowers are suitable for reproducing in bobbin lace and from the variety of patterns here it should be possible to extend the range indefinitely by matching up the petals and making slight alterations. For instance, one student had a large collection of fuchsias and intended to copy them all in lace! I have a watercolour by Patience Pearson of bindweed, nightshade and berries. I had copied the flowers in Honiton (with help from Susanne Thompson) then made them in 3D, twining around inside a glass dome - together they make an interesting corner.

Lacemaking, like other hobbies, leads one down all sorts of interesting avenues and here is another - the study of elementary botany. It is obviously necessary to know how many petals to make, how they are arranged and whether there are stamens or bracts - the use of a good magnifying glass reveals untold treasures. May your experiments bring you endless delight.

EQUIPMENT

40cm or 46cm (16″ or 18″) dressed pillow, pricking and fine pins
fine **lacquered** electronic or fisherman's wire, gauge 38 (0.15mm), pink
plasticised stem wire, gauge 19, 22 or 26 (from florist) depending on the flower
green stem tape
stamens if needed (florist or craft shop)
florist's ribbon (leaf green)
narrow double-sided sticky tape
sharp scissors
old scissors (not sharp) for bowing off and cutting wire
small pliers or tweezers
Sylko (cotton) or DMC Broder Machine 30 (see page 61)

ABBREVIATIONS and GLOSSARY

prs - pairs
st - stitch
LH - left hand
RH - right hand
cl.st - cloth stitch
h.st - half stitch
d/s/tape - double-sided sticky tape
Broder m/c - DMC Broder Machine thread
w - lacquered wire, gauge 38
B/T - Basic Techniques, page 7

Petals - main coloured parts of flower
Sepals - these form a ring round the base of the flower, usually green but sometimes the same colour as the petals (orchid, fuchsia)
Calyx - the sepals as a whole, usually when they are joined (pinks, snowdrop)
Bracts - like leaves, just below the flower (pinks, anemone)
Spathe - a sheath enclosing the bud which splits when the flower opens, sometimes drops away but often stands up behind the flower (snowdrop, snowflake)
Style and stigma - female filaments in the centre of the flower
Stamens - male filaments and sac containing pollen, surrounding the style
Pod or capsule - seed vessel

GENERAL NOTES

Making simple 3D flowers in plain cloth stitch or half stitch is within the scope of the near beginner in lace. "Bowing off' and making up takes a little perseverance - nimble fingers are an asset, but practice makes perfect as in any craft. Some people say the constant starting and finishing is tedious but in the section on Basic Techniques there are time-saving hints which reduce the chore to a minimum.

Ways of creating different effects by using a variety of stitches and twists are indicated in the patterns. Covered wire in different colours is available from craft shops, but the finest you can buy is about gauge 30 which makes some flowers appear clumsy. I find that electronic lacquered wire, gauge 38, gives just enough stiffness without being too obvious. It is available from specialist electronic and fishermen's suppliers.

The rich vibrant colours in Nature are not achieved by solid tones. Examination of any flower through a good magnifying glass reveals numerous veins in a variety of shades or even different colours. A good example of this is seen in the inner petal of the Fuchsia (pattern 7, page 28), where royal blue, ruby red and violet combine to make a glowing purple. Leaves, too, vary both in colour and shading. Look at a rose leaf; you can use a brown thread each side of the central vein and also for the outer passives to get the effect of the brown tinged edge, together with different shades of green to represent the highlights. A list of most of the colours I have used is on page 61. The numbers are for cotton Sylko and DMC Broder Machine 30.
Mettler 30 may also be used but is not available everywhere.

Tubular flowers will normally support themselves without wire, although larger or longer petals benefit from a little stiffening, as in the Gentian. Arrangements of large round flowers (e.g. roses in a bouquet or posy) need smaller pointed flowers to set them off and give variety so I have included two which can be used for this purpose - Kaffir Lily and Freesia. There is also a set of Butterflies to have fun with.

To create your own pattern, take a flower to pieces and draw round the petal. Rule a line from the tip to the base and on this mark dots 2mm apart. Draw lines through these to the outline and where the lines cross you have the pin-hole points. You can of course, use 2mm graph paper if you have it, ignoring the vertical lines. Transfer this pattern on to glazed pricking card. Note the number of petals and how they are arranged, how many stamens there are and how the flowers are attached to the stem (a rough sketch is most useful). Compare the width of the petal with a similar one in this collection to give you an idea as to the number of bobbins to use.

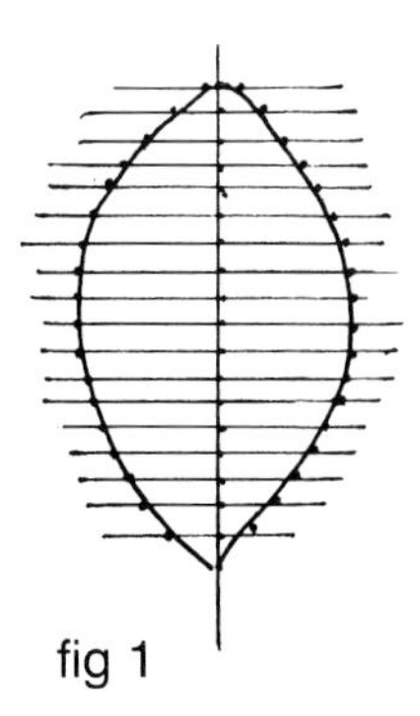
fig 1

Finally, a small bobbin winder is handy to have in your lace bag and you will find instructions how to make one at the end of the book.

BASIC TECHNIQUES

These apply to both simple and wired flowers, with slight individual variations. It would be a good idea to keep a bookmark at this page so that it can be easily referred to while working the patterns.
The pricking patterns are clear and uncomplicated so they should be easy to trace.
Do use proper glazed pricking card - it needs to be good for many times.

For larger flowers a pillow big enough to swing up to 34 prs of bobbins is necessary - a 40cm (16´´) or 46cm (18´´) round pillow is ideal.

1. **Bobbins** - one of each pr to be **fully wound**, the other to have about 40cm (16´´) - the 'sparse bobbin'. The full bobbins take turns as workers in subsequent petals, the rest are passives and use very little thread.

2. **Hang all prs open** round the top pin, with 2 full bobbins on the worker side (*fig 2*). Mix the shades as you hang in. If you wish to use a few good extra colours in a finer thread increase the number of passives slightly. Variegated thread is good for passives but for the workers it must be organised with forethought. Keep the passives pulled down well in the first few rows.

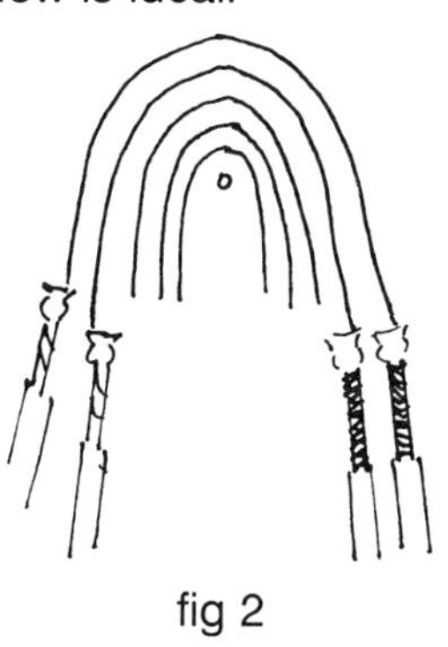

fig 2

3. **Twist all prs twice.**

4. **Wired petals only.** With a slip-knot attach about 35cm (14´´) lacquered electronic wire, gauge 38, to a pr of bobbins so that they hang down from the top pin level with and outside the rest. Do not use more than this as the wire does not slip through a a half-hitch easily. (*fig 3a*).

   Place the RH wire towards the back of the pillow, say about 2 o'clock, and anchor it with a berry pin through the spangle.

   Now weave the LH wire to the R through all the bobbins **except the workers at the end,** (*fig 3b*).

   Take the latter to the L in cloth st, using the wire and its neighbour as the first passive pr. At the LH side there will be an odd thread - release the other wired bobbin and bring it round on the outside to make up the pair. Work through this (*fig 3c*).

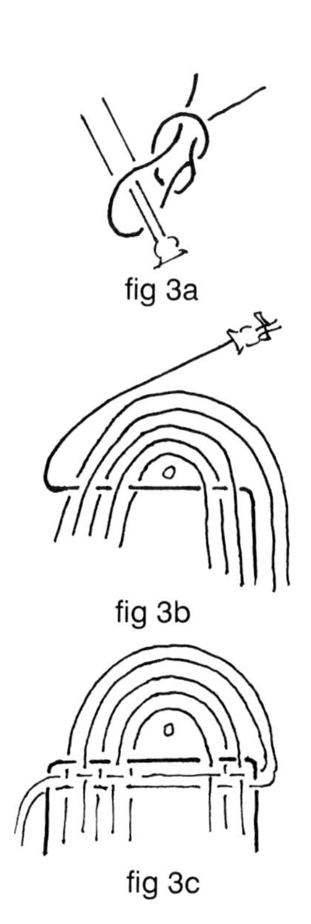

fig 3a

fig 3b

fig 3c

Most patterns in this collection start from the RH side and work the first row to the L, but where the first row starts from L to R the above instructions are reversed (eg. Pattern 8, the Iris, winged petal, and opposite wings of the Butterflies).

The edge stitch is cloth st and 2 twists unless otherwise stated. Complete the petal, keeping the wire as the outside passive throughout. This is now counted with its partner as a pair.

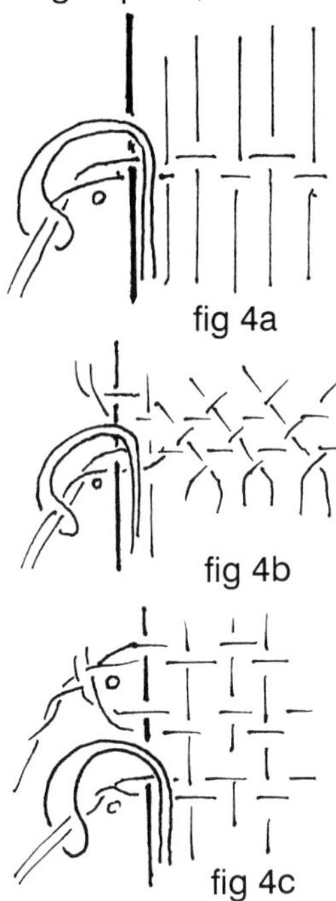
fig 4a
fig 4b
fig 4c

5. **Adding new pairs** where the petal widens excessively. Set the edge pin, but before making up the stitch, slide the new pr (one bobbin in each hand) under the workers, bring them together and take them round the outside pin, laying them down **between** the 2 outer passive threads, thus keeping one continuous wire on the outside (*fig 4a*). Two prs can be added in turn at the same time if necessary.

   Fig 4a shows a pr added to **cloth st**; *fig 4b* is a **half-st** petal, but the edge prs are always worked in cloth st; *fig 4c* is a **'straight edge'** - prs are added before the edge st is made up.

6. **Reducing** where the petal narrows excessively. Lay threads to the back of the work to be cut off later (but not 2 threads together as this might be obvious). Do not do this too soon - wait until the cloth is tight enough for the loss to be unnoticeable. Reducing is not necessary in half st as the threads close in together.

7. **Work to the bottom** of the petal. Cut off the wires but do not touch the laid back prs until after stage 8.

8. **Bundle and bunch** the remaining threads crossing the outside prs under the bunch, having lengthened these to at least 15cm (6′′).

   Tie these singly over the top in a reef knot with an extra twist on the first half, as in tying children's shoelaces (L over R and over again, R over L). This prevents the knot loosening before the second half is tied. Hold the bobbins by the neck so that the spangle leads through the loop - this is why you need plenty of thread for the operation (*fig 5a and 5b).*

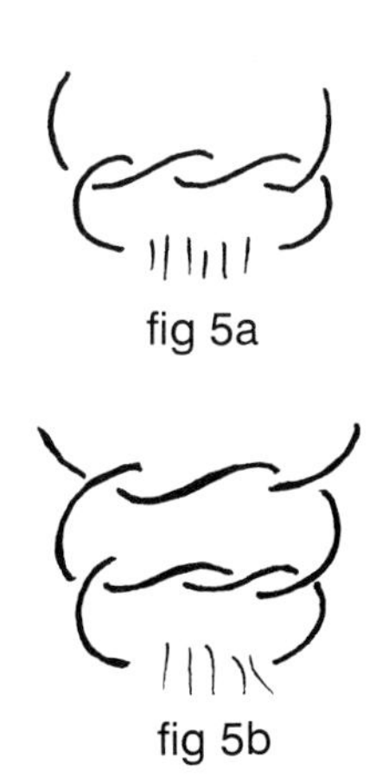
fig 5a
fig 5b

9. **Take out the top pin** and replace it under the lace ready for the next petal. Bring down the laid back prs.

10. Bowing off, using non-sharp scissors, (*fig 6*).

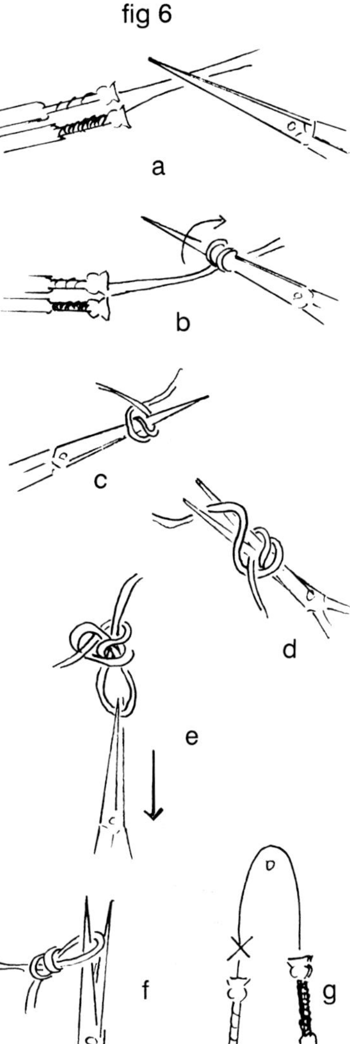

a Take **any one full bobbin** with **any one sparse bobbin** in one hand, threads extended from the pillow.

b Place the closed blades of the scissors over the threads, point towards the bobbins. Wind the thread once (or twice, which I prefer) round the blades, away from you.

c Turn the point towards the pillow. There is now a twist on the threads below the scissors.

d Open the blades slightly to clasp the lace threads from below. **RELAX !**

e Close the scissors (this is why they must not be sharp) and draw the threads through the ring formed round the blades, easing it off the point and onto the lace threads. Keep everything loose, not tense.

f Gently pull the bobbins to tighten the knot, cut the loop, draw out the threads, separate the bobbins, and you will find the pair is again joined ready for work.

g Wind the knot back towards the sparse bobbin and **immediately** hang the bobbins over the top pin (B/T.2.). Twist all twice, remembering to have 2 full bobbins on the worker side. Do not remove the rest of the pins until all the threads are bowed off. A fresh pr of wired bobbins will be required.

There will be knots on half the bobbins - **make sure these hang down at least 5cm (2´´) below the bottom of the pattern,** especially the ones attached to the worker pr. These knotted threads are all passives and will not come into the lace. Check this after the 3rd row - this is your last opportunity to adjust them.

If you have no blunt scissors, a crochet hook or tweezers can be used to bow off but the loop will need to be snipped separately. The threads from the laid back prs can now be trimmed close to the work.

You will have noticed that most of the foregoing techniques are adaptations from Bedfordshire and Honiton laces.

11. Make the number of petals required for the flower.

ASSEMBLING

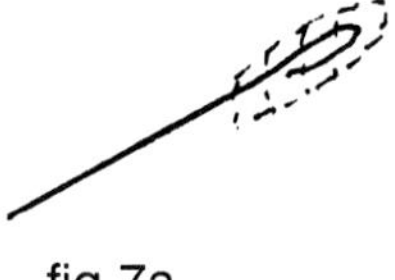

fig 7a

12. **Using plasticised stem wire**, fold over the tip and press a small piece of green stem tape or narrow double-sided sticky tape onto this, to prevent the petals sliding off if you are too energetic (*fig 7a*).

    Gauge 26 stem wire is adequate for most flowers, but heavier ones such as the Bush Rose, Iris, Carnation or Cyclamen, on long single stems are better with 19, 22 or even double 26.

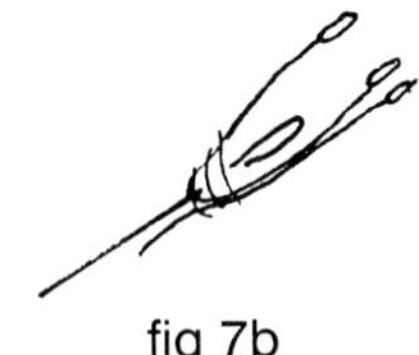

fig 7b

13. **Take a needle threaded with cotton** the same colour as the flower and bind on the stamens if these are needed, (*fig 7b*), securing with a half-hitch or two, (a figure of 8 round the 2nd finger, *fig 7c*). Do the same with the petals. The needle is not essential but I find it useful sometimes to slip a stitch through the petal. Finish off securely.

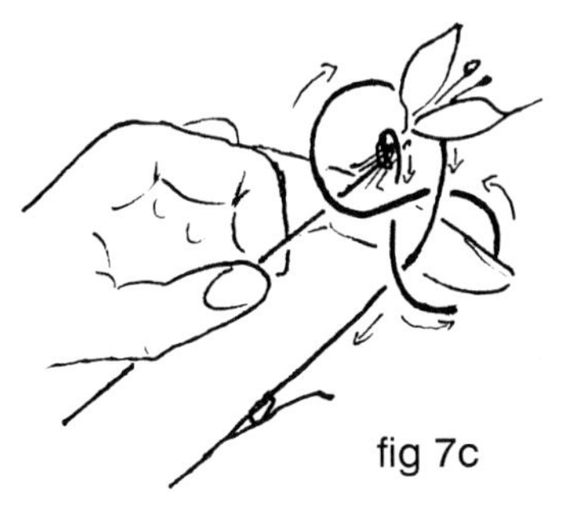

fig 7c

14. **Trim ends** to about 15mm (1/2″), graduated.

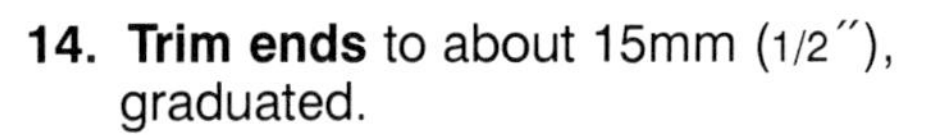

15. **Place the sepals** round the base of the petals and bind them on - here again a small piece of sticky tape will help to keep them firm while you wind the thread round (*fig 7d*).

fig 7d

16. **Take 10cm (4″) of green stem tape** and cut this in half lengthwise - this makes a neater and finer stem than using the full width, (the same applies to wider sticky tape). Start binding the calyx just over the base of the sepals. Stretch the tape gently, holding it close to the flower, and make sure all the loose ends are covered. **Now hold the tape onto the stem firmly** with finger and thumb of one hand while the other finger and thumb twists the stem round, the tape thus being slightly stretched and binding itself in a spiral to cover the full length (*fig 7e*).

    Incorporate leaves where required.

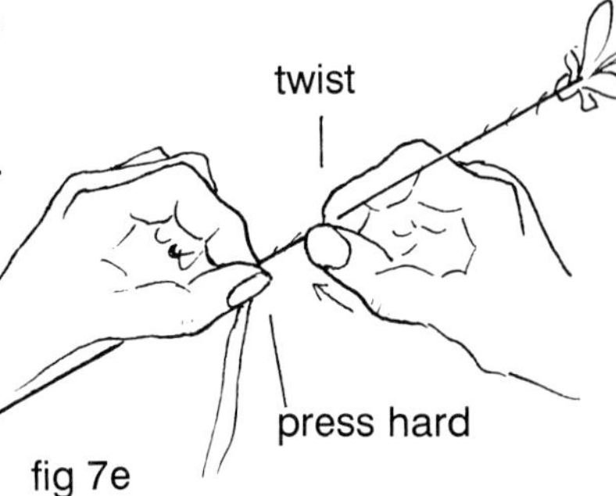

fig 7e

17. **Making up a bouquet or posy.** 'Our Bouquet' by the Itchen Valley Lacemakers has some excellent instructions but unfortunately this is out of print. Floristry books should be available in the Public Library, or better still consult a friendly florist.

LEAVES

Leaves may be worked in lace, cut from florist's ribbon or bought ready made in silk or latex. These can be trimmed to any appropriate shape, as illustrated.

LACE LEAVES follow the same basic techniques as flower petals, B/T 1-3, 5-11. The green stem wire is incorporated as the work proceeds, representing the central vein, either passing between the worker threads (under the L when working to the R and under the R when working to the L, so that it passes down through alternate threads), or used like a gimp, with twists on each side. The wire is anchored by a small hook over the top pin at the beginning of the work (*figs 8a &b*).

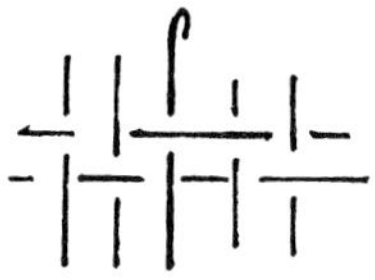

fig 8a

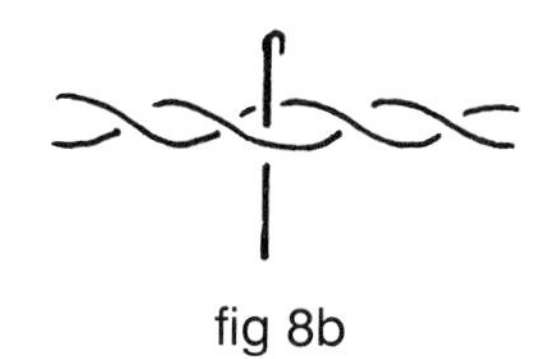

fig 8b

Shading is made by the use of lighter green passives in different places, but I think the most effective way is to have one side of the midrib light and the other dark (*fig 8c*). A lighter or darker worker pr also alters the tone of different leaves. Another variation can be made by working cloth st on one half and half-st on the other, with the wire midrib as the dividing line.

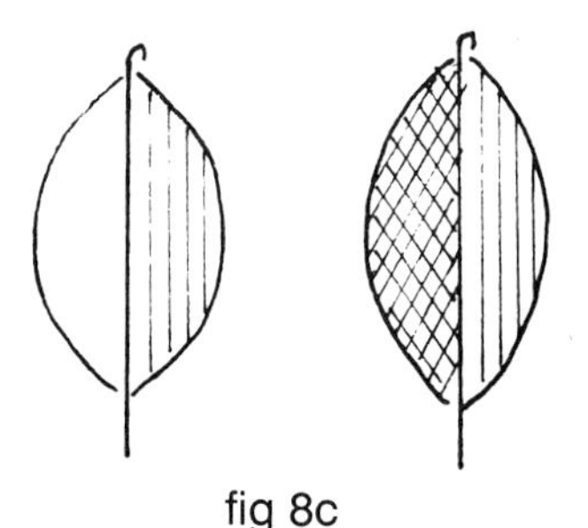

fig 8c

VEINS can be indicated with a needle and thread after the leaf is completed or worked as follows:

Pinnate leaves - rose, fuchsia etc (*fig 8d)*
Start with 5prs Dark Olive and 4prs Light Olive round the top pin (B/T 1 & 2). There will be equal colours both sides, so if you want all dark on one side it will be necessary at this point to weave them through to the other side as in half a spider.

Turn over the end of a green stem wire and hook this over the top pin. Cloth st to the first vein mark, adding prs as the leaf progresses, and passing the centre wire between the workers.

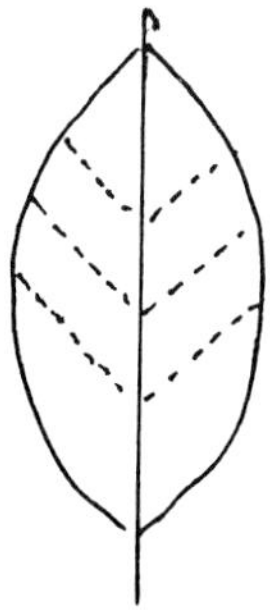

fig 8d

Row 1 (to R) L edge st, twist workers twice, cloth st, twist LH passives twice. Cloth st to centre, pass wire between workers, cloth st to RH side, edge st.

Row 2 (to L) Twist workers twice, cloth st, twist RH passives twice, cloth st to L as far as the twisted passive. Twist worker and RH passive twice, cloth st to end of row.

Row 3 (to R) Cloth st to the twisted passive, cloth st through it, twist twice, cloth st, twist the LH passive twice. Cloth st to the next twisted passive, twist worker and passive twice. Cloth st to end.

Row 4 (to L) Cloth st to twisted passive, cloth st, twist worker twice, cloth st, twist RH passive twice. Cloth st to next twisted passive, twist worker and RH passive twice. Cloth st to end.

Repeat rows 3 and 4, bringing the twists one stitch nearer the centre on each row until they arrive at the wire, when it is time to start again at row 1. The effect is veins of diagonal holes.

This may sound rather complicated - perhaps the diagram will clarify it.

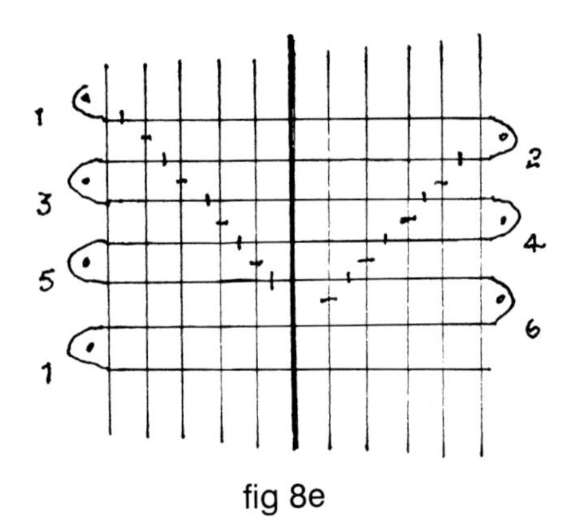

fig 8e

Finish leaf as flower petal, B/T 6-9

Lanceolate leaves - Kaffir Lily, Freesia, most bulbs.

The veins rise parallel from the base and this is easily indicated by single twists on the workers directly under each other, ie. ladders. The central wire enables the leaf to be bent and twisted in a natural way. However, leaves cut from florist's ribbon are very effective and provide another texture.

RIBBON LEAVES

Cut out the shape in green florist's ribbon. Place this on folded newspaper and mark the veins with a smooth instrument (the handle of a teaspoon or top of a biro cap). Turn wrong side up. Press full-width double-sided sticky tape down the centre line. Bind a short stem wire with stem tape, press the top part of this onto the leaf over the sticky tape, cover again with d/s tape and then with full-width stem tape, pressed in well. Turn right way up and gently bend into a natural shape.

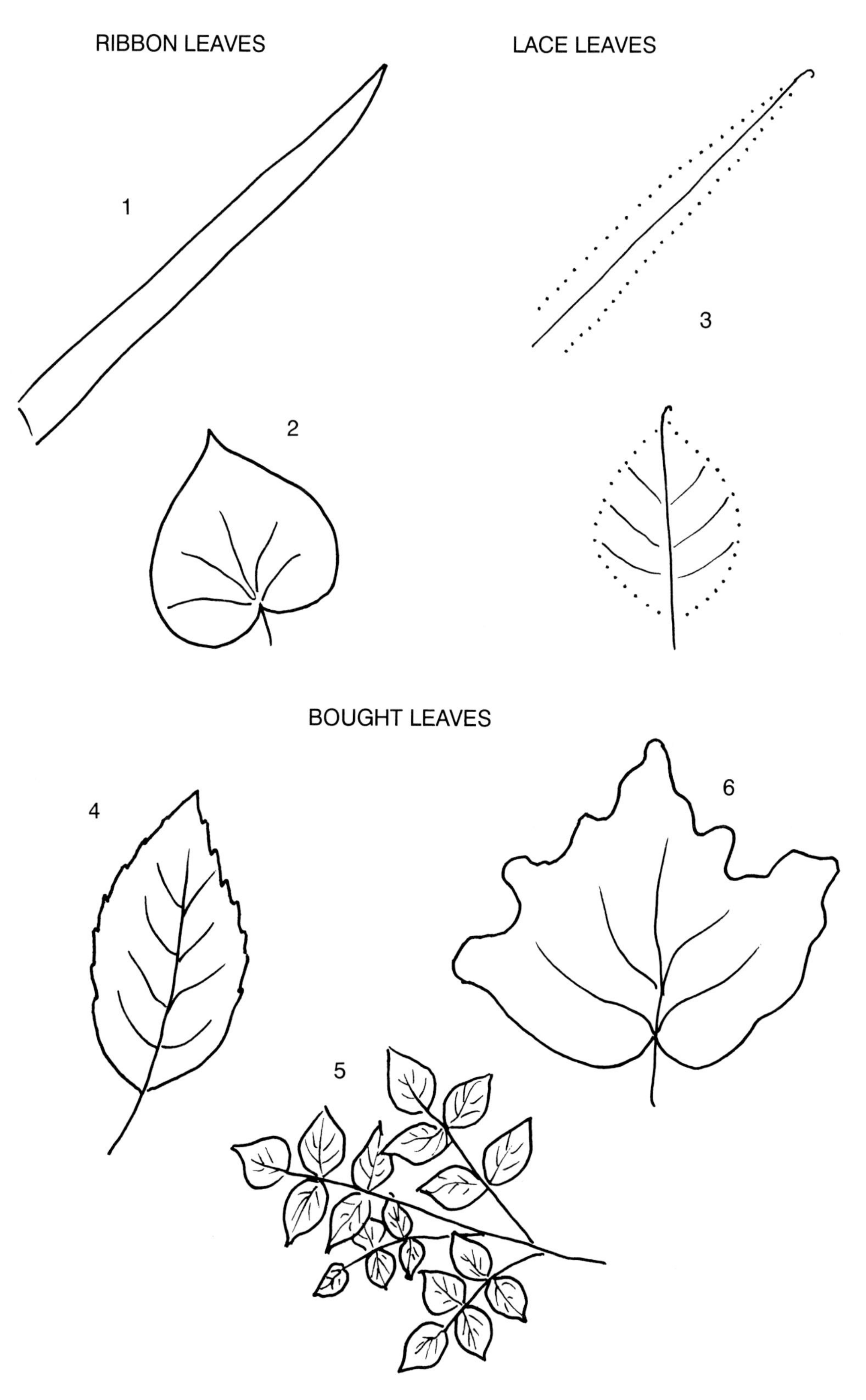
RIBBON LEAVES
LACE LEAVES
1
3
2
BOUGHT LEAVES
6
4
5

FLOWERS

PATTERN 1

PATIO ROSE 'Sweet magic'
15 prs toning colours, cotton Sylko or DMC Broder Machine 30
suggestions - 7 prs Sunrise, 3 prs Flame, 3 prs Tangerine, 2 prs Lemon
8 prs Light Olive for sepals
1 pr lacquered electronic wire, gauge 38
plasticised green stem wire, gauge 22 or 26
green stem tape
narrow double-sided sticky tape
spray of small bought rose leaves

This is a quickly made and simple introduction to wired flowers.

Read the Basic Techniques pages first.

PETALS 15prs, plus wire
Hang 7 prs open round the top pin, keeping darker colours in the centre and grading the others out to the edge. Remember to have **two full bobbins** of the pale Sunrise at the RH side for the workers (*fig 2*). Twist all twice.
Attach the wire to a spare pr of bobbins (*fig 3a*) and hang on the top pin, supporting the RH bobbin at the back of the pillow at about 2 o'clock.
Weave the LH wire through all except the workers (*fig 3b*).
Now cloth st these workers to L, starting with the wire and its partner. At the end there will be an odd bobbin, so release the other wire and bring it down to the outside L, where it is used with the odd passive to complete the cloth st row (*fig 3c*).
The edge st is cloth st and 2 twists.
Add prs each side until all are in use (B/T5, *fig 4a*). Continue in cloth st, keeping the wire as the outer passive thread, to x-x when prs may be laid back until 7 prs remain. Follow B/T 7-11. Make at least 5.

SEPALS 8 prs
5 sepals are worked in Olive Green, with no edging wire. Bow off in 2 bunches (B/T 8)

ASSEMBLING
Follow B/T stages 12-16, (*figs 7a-d*), padding the hooked stem wire with a small cone of cottonwool to fill out the bud. Around this fold the first dark petal, stitch the edges together at the top, then add the rest of the petals, each one overlapping one edge of the previous one.
Any number over 7 will produce an attractive open rose - for this the sepals turn back, whereas in the bud they cling close around it.
When all the petals and sepals are securely attached to the top of the stem wire, trim the ends to 15mm (1/2´´) and bind these with d/s tape, then with half-width stem tape to the end of the stem (B/T 16).

Arrange a few buds and flowers in front of a bought spray of small rose leaves.

PATTERN 1 PATIO ROSE

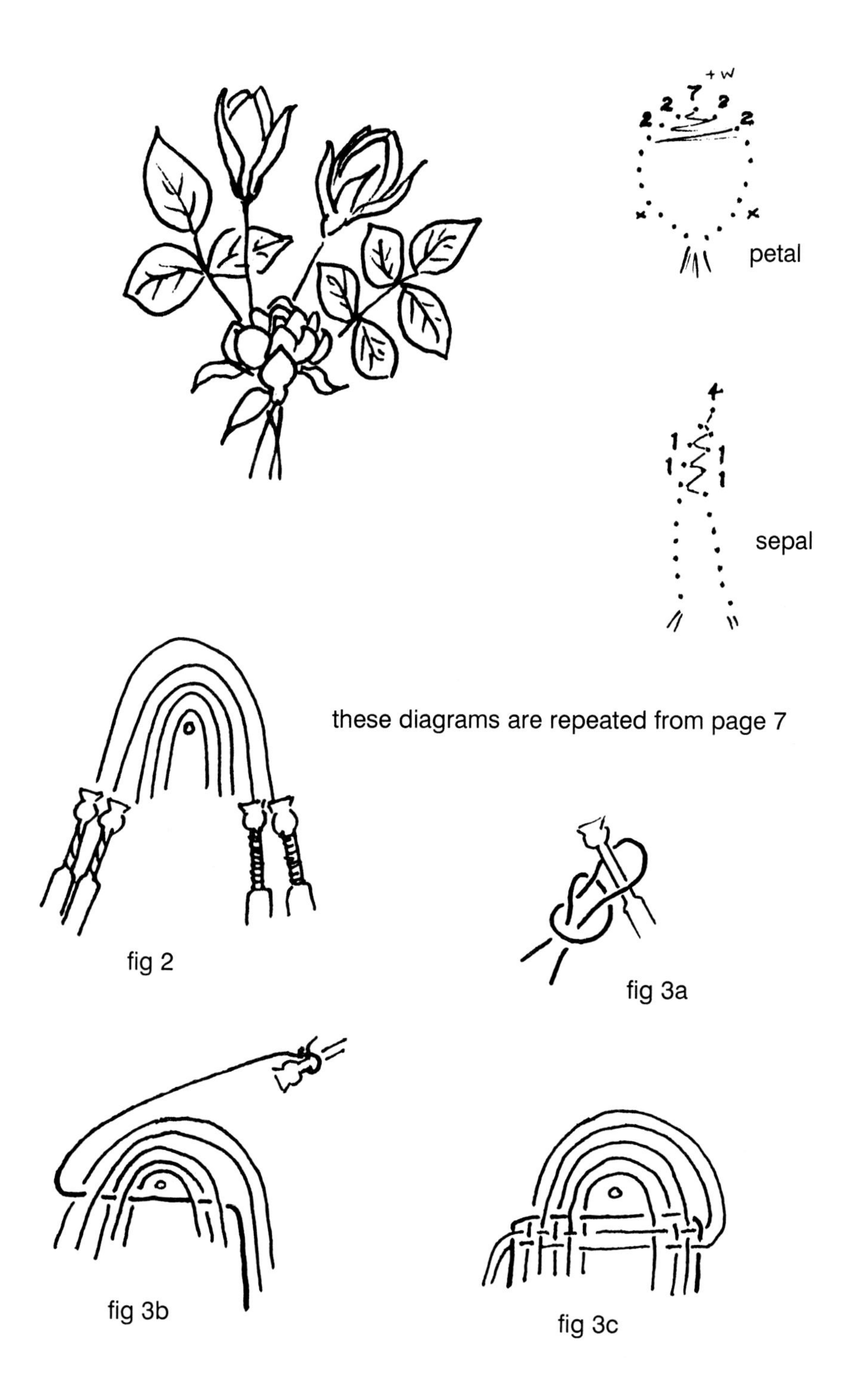

these diagrams are repeated from page 7

fig 2

fig 3a

fig 3b

fig 3c

PATTERN 2

BUSH ROSE - 'Fragrant Cloud'
At least 32 prs in 3 toning colours

Suggestions - Sylko - Ruby, Red Salmon, Coral Pink
and for leaves - Light Olive and Dark Olive
1 pr fine electronic wire, gauge 38

plasticised green stem wire, gauge 19 for this heavier flower.
green stem tape
double sided sticky tape

SMALL PETAL B/T 1-11 11prs, increasing to 16, plus wire.
Edge st is cloth st and 2 twists. Use all dark colour for the two centre petals.
Substitute the medium colour for the 4 outer passives each side of the next 3 petals, graduating them by mixing the threads outwards from the centre so that subsequent petals are lighter. Reduce to 10 prs.
Make 5 petals.

MEDIUM PETAL 11 prs, increasing to 25, plus wire
Start shading now - use a dark worker with several dark passives in the centre, then medium and dark threads alternately, and finally all medium on the outside.
Use medium added prs. Reduce to 10 prs towards the end by taking out the darker shades.
Make 7 petals like this, then change to medium workers for the next 3 petals, introducing light prs at the outer edges.
Tie off in 2 bunches.
Make 10 petals.

LARGE PETAL 11 prs, increasing to 32, plus wire
Work as for medium petal, shading the darkest colours towards the middle and introducing more light threads, with a medium colour for the worker.
Make 5 petals.

SEPAL B/T 1-3, 5-11 4 prs increasing to 9. No wire.
Use Light Olive worker, 2 Light Olive passives with 1 Dark Olive in the middle. Add 5 Light Olives as indicated on the pattern. Tie off in 2 bunches.
Make 5.

ASSEMBLING B/T 12-16

LEAVES can be bought or worked in lace.
For lace leaves start with 9 prs, adding 2 prs each side up to 21. Use stem wire for the midrib (Page 11) and follow *fig 8e* (page 12) for integral veining.

PATTERN 2 BUSH ROSE

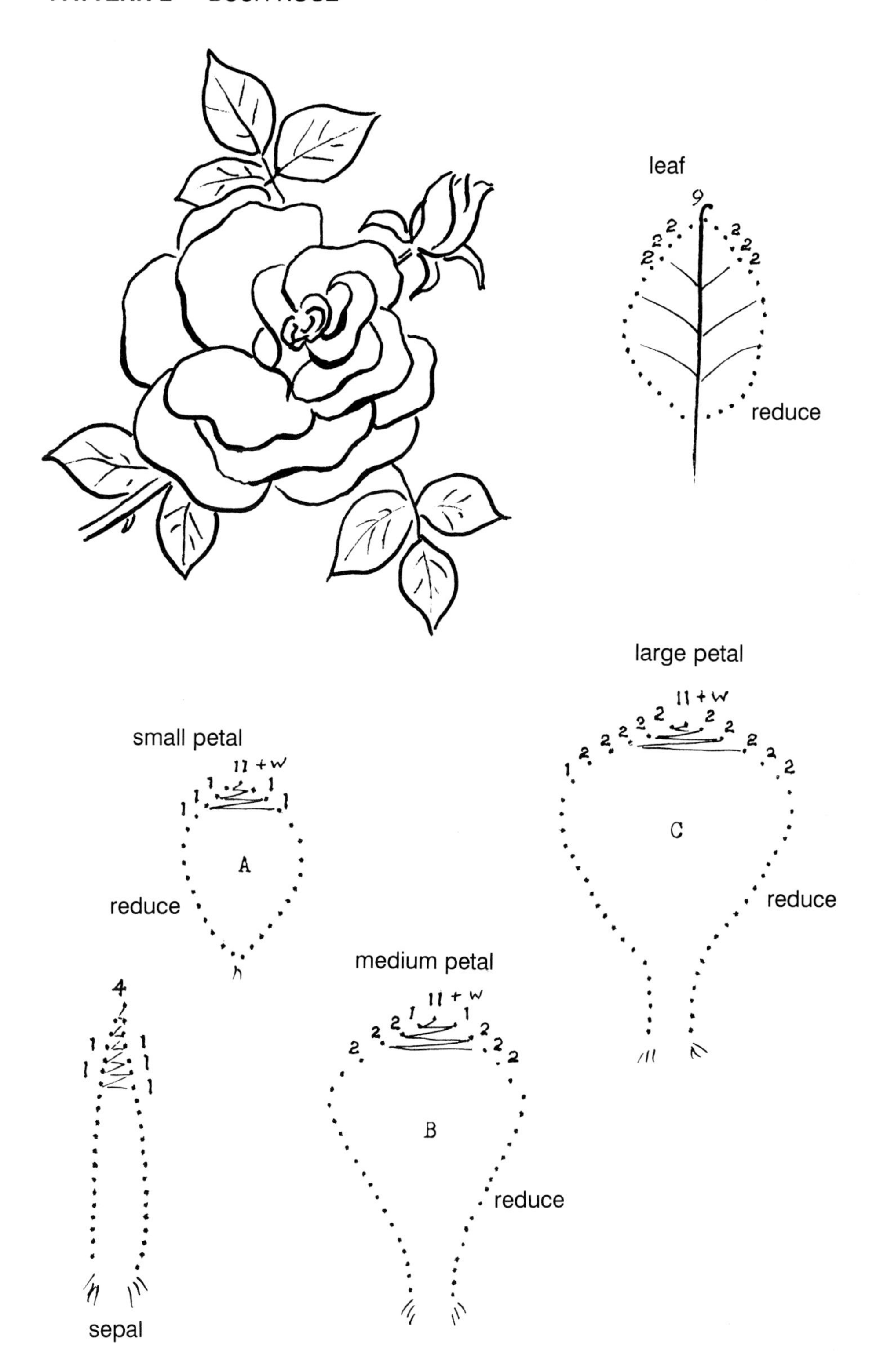

PATTERN 3

GARDENIA - Cape Jasmine
26 prs Sylko, mostly white with a few passives of white Broder m/c 30 which is a softer white than Sylko
21 prs Light and Dark Olive for leaves

fine electronic lacquered wire
green stem wire
green stem tape
double-sided sticky tape

This is worked in much the same way as the roses. The leaf is like a slightly elongated rose leaf. For the petal I used the pink fine wire and coated the middle 10cm (4´´) of the working part with Tippex, doing several at a time by suspending the bobbins across a box. This was quite effective, although the fine wire is hardly noticeable anyway.
Although one thinks of a gardenia as white, plain white Sylko is rather stark. Add a few prs of passives in white Broder m/c 30 and the result is a softer natural look.

SMALL PETAL B/T 1-11
15 prs plus wire
Start with 8 prs and wire, increasing to 15. Reduce to 10 towards the end.
Make 5.

MEDIUM PETAL 22 prs plus wire
As small petal, starting with 10 prs and adding 2 prs at a time (*fig 4a*, page 8)
Reduce to 10 at the end. Tie off in 2 bunches.
Make 5

LARGE PETAL 26 prs plus wire
As medium petal.
Make 5 or more.

LEAVES 22 prs. See *fig 8e* (page 12) for veining. Start with 11, adding prs each side. The green stem wire is hooked over the top pin and forms the midrib. Reduce to 10 prs.
Make 10, using a Light Olive worker for 5 - these are the younger ones growing nearest the flower. Use a Dark Olive worker for the other 5 which form the outer rosette. Other greens can be included as occasional passives to vary the shading.

ASSEMBLING B/T 13-15

As no stamens are required, press a small piece of d/sided tape and stem tape onto the bent-over tip of the stem wire and arrange the small petals round it, squeezing the first one together to hide the green tip. Follow with the other petals in sequence, then the light leaves and finally the dark leaves.
As all the stems are close together they can be bound together with d/s tape to form a short-stemmed corsage and finished with stem tape.

PATTERN 3 GARDENIA

small petal

leaf

medium petal

large petal

PATTERN 4

BETTY'S ORCHIDS (Adelaide)
There are many different types of orchids to choose from - I have a friend who grows 28 varieties on her patio and she allowed me to take one to pieces for a pattern. This will serve for Rosarica Majestic (pink) and Swallow Daffodil (yellow). Different treatments result in two different types.

ROSARICA MAJESTIC

At least 30 prs in toning colours - Red Salmon, Pale Rose and a few prs of Ruby and yellow for the honey guides.

fine electronic wire in pink
green plasticised stem wire, gauge 19
brown stem tape
double-sided sticky tape
2 large pearl stamens

Lip (pricking 1) 22 prs plus wire
This is worked in two sections then joined down the centre, A - A
Start with 8 prs Red Salmon and 1 pr fine wire. Keep an eye on *fig 9a* opposite.
Cloth st to row 3 and add 1 pr Ruby and 1 pr Pale Rose near the straight edge **(hang on a support pin above the work)**, release after 3 rows and ease gently into place. Be careful not to put pressure on these passives when working the rest of the petal or you will have an unsightly hole. In subsequent rows add more Ruby prs in the same way, getting nearer the outside edge, also one or two Yellow prs towards the middle.
After a few more rows start adding Pale Rose prs near the straight edge until all 22 prs are incorporated. At B start throwing back some of the darker prs in the middle but leave at least 2 of the Ruby prs nearest the straight edge till the end (these are all cut off close after completion). Reduce to about 10 prs.

Sew the two petals together along the straight edge A to A.

Hood (pricking 2) 30 prs plus wire (*fig 9b*)
Start with 10 prs, using a Red Salmon worker and Pale Rose passives. Cloth st 3 rows then add 2 prs Red Salmon in the centre (over a support pin as above), continue adding these in the centre for 4 rows, then commence a ladder on each side of the centre pr (twist worker, cloth st, twist worker). Add pale prs on each edge until all prs are included. Reduce prs where pattern narrows (B/T6).
Bow off and trim the laid back threads close to the work.
Stitch lip and hood together B_1 to B_1 and B_2 to B_2 to form a short tube.

Backing petals (pricking 3) 22 prs and wire for upper side petals

(pricking 4) 26 prs and wire for lower side petals

(pricking 5) 30 prs and wire for top petal

Start with 10 prs and wire. Use a pale worker and passives, gradually adding in deeper pink. After 6 rows start a ladder in the centre (twist worker

PATTERN 4 BETTY'S ORCHIDS

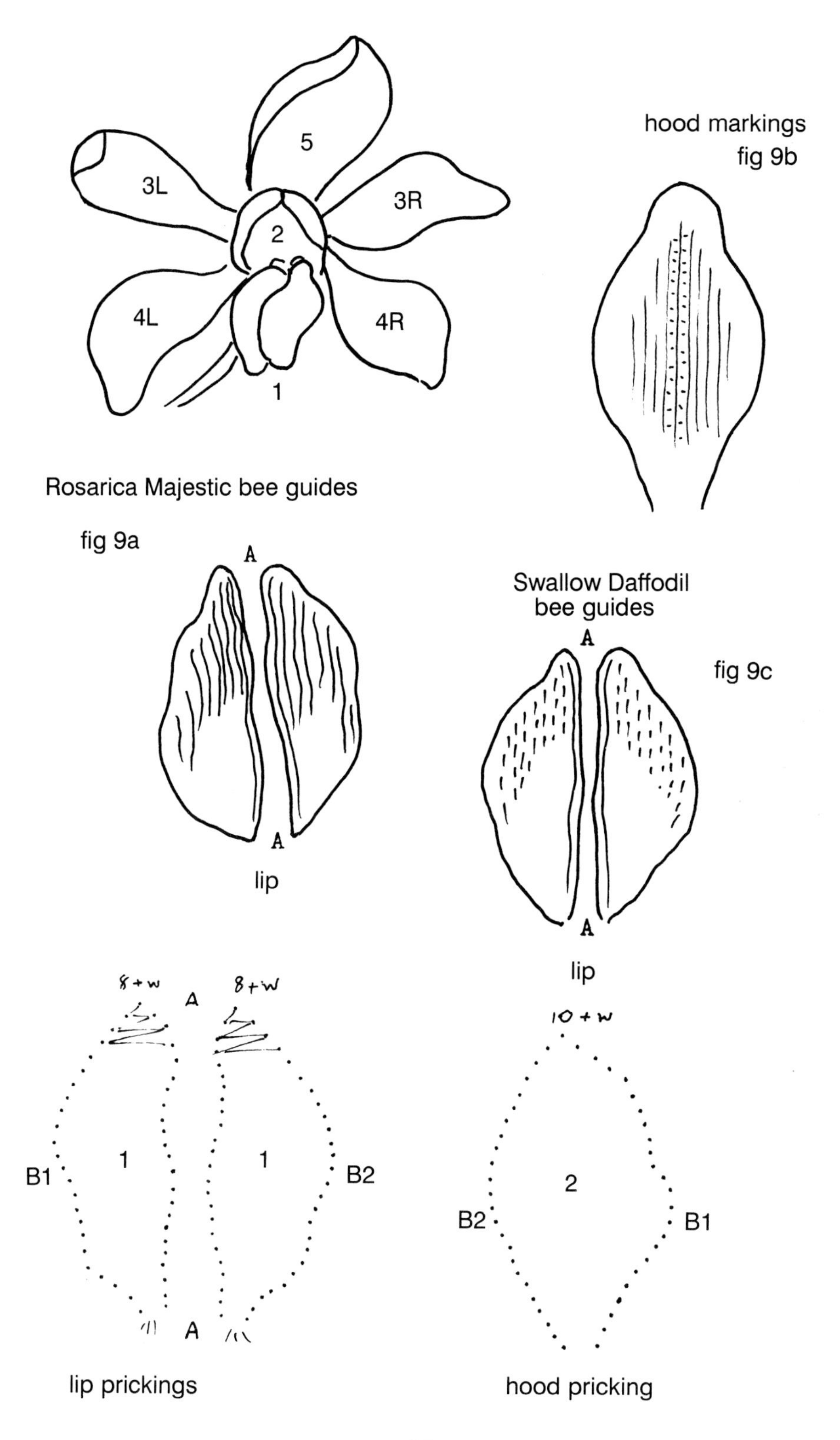

then in the next 2 rows twist twice, and after that 3 times until the petal starts to narrow, when the twists are reduced and finally omitted).

ORCHID - SWALLOW DAFFODIL

Follow the instructions for the pink orchid but use pale yellow, cream and buff Sylko. Mix the passives to give variety of shading and work in cloth st throughout, with no ladders.

The Lip has dark red broken honey guides in a mainly yellow background (*fig 9c*, page 21).
To achieve this use several Ruby passives in a staggered formation - every few rows pass them over their adjacent yellow neighbours, bringing them into the work again one or two stitches further along the row. The exception is the dark line next to the straight edge A - A which carries straight down to the end of the petal. Sew the two petals along the straight edge.

ASSEMBLING BOTH FLOWERS B/T 12-16

Tie the 2 large pearl stamens on top of the stem wire and insert into the tube of lip and hood so they protrude level with the stitching.

Behind the tube bind on the 2 upper side petals, then the lower side petals and finally the top petal at the back of all (these three are actually coloured sepals).

Trim the thread ends to 1-2cm (1/2″), graduated, and finish off with brown stem tape. Bend the lip forward and the hood back, with its sides curving inwards.

petal prickings

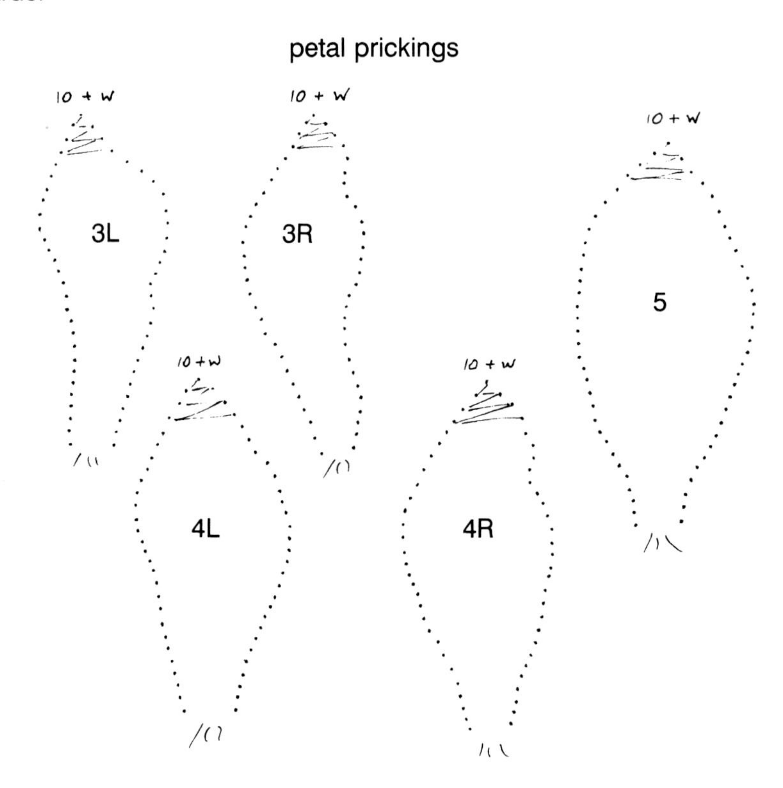

PATTERN 5

CARNATION and PINKS - Dianthus
up to 30 prs toning colours. (Variegated thread may be used to advantage, but only for the passives)
fine lacquered wire, gauge 38, pink
plasticised stem wire, gauge 19 or 22
blue-green stem tape
blue-green florist's ribbon
double-sided sticky tape
stamens for the pinks

CARNATION B/T 1-11 30prs, 1 pr fine wire
I used all the toning reds I could find in my sewing box -
Poppy for the workers, Ruby, Scarlet, Light Scarlet, Frivolous Pink and Flame, resulting in a vibrant red carnation almost indistinguishable from the real flower.
Try to graduate the tones from darkest in the centre to lighter outer petals.

Petal 1 10 prs darkest colours. Cloth st, no wire.
Make 5

Petal 2 13 prs, 1 pr wire.

To simulate the deckle edge, start by making **false picots** on the top 4 pins:-
Hang 1 light and 1 darker pr open round the pin (B/T 2), with an extra pr on the RH pin, (arrange these so that **2 full lighter bobbins** are at this end, placed to one side).
Twist each adjacent couple 3 times with an extra twist on the LH pr; close the pin with cloth st. This should result in alternate colours along the row.
Weave the wire through all these (B/T 4) and tie each pr in a single knot to enclose and hold the wire near to the picots. Now use the 2 full RH bobbins as workers in cloth st across the row.
Edge st is cloth st and 3 twists, pin, cloth st.
Add new prs at each end as indicated (B/T 5), making sure the wire is still the outside passive.
After this twist only twice at the edge as the petal sides are straight.
Ladders add interest in these wider petals - at the centre twist the workers once, then at the same place in the next row twist twice. Now start other ladders equidistant from this - say every 3 stitches - and continue until the petal narrows, when they are reduced then discontinued. Prs are then laid back until about 8 remain.
As the petal starts in a different way from the norm, when bowing off wind the threads close to the bobbins and lay them down carefully in pairs, or put them in a sectioned bobbin case.
Make 5

Petal 3 24 prs mixed reds, 1 pr wire
Work as petal 2. Make 5

Petal 4 30 prs mixed reds, 1 pr wire
Work as petal 2, using the top 5 pins for false picots.
Make about 15-20, using a slightly lighter worker for the outer petals.

The flower I examined had 70 petals, but 35 will do!
ASSEMBLING as B/T 12-16, overlapping each petal in turn.
Trim ends to 2cm (3/4´´) for the long calyx, bind with d/s tape then stem tape.
About 2.5cm (1´´) below the calyx add in 2 small grass-like bracts of florist's ribbon on opposite sides of the stem, then a few longer ones further down the stem for leaves.
The petals can be crimped with small pliers or pastry crimpers.

MODERN PINK - "Doris"
30 prs mixed pinks - Pale Rose, Fiesta Pink, Red Salmon and Ruby
fine wire
3 beheaded stamens

Tiny inner petal - pricking 1
5 prs lightest colour, including worker
5 prs medium colour
Cloth st, no wire. Make 5

Medium petal - pricking 3
12 prs light pink
11 prs darker pink
1 full pr dark ruby
1 pr fine wire

Follow working instructions for Carnation petal 2. At A introduce the Ruby pr as workers for 5 rows, then discard these and change back to a light worker.
Make 5.

Large petal - pricking 4
13 prs light
13 prs medium
1 full pr dark ruby
1 pr fine wire

Work as for medium petal, using the top 5 pins for false picots and again adding ruby workers for 5 rows.
Make at least 7. **Assemble** as carnation, starting with the stamens.

SINGLE PINK - pricking 2
13 prs white Sylko
Ruby or Cerise for needle-worked blotch
fine wire
10 beheaded stamens

Make 5 petals in white. Before assembling, work the dark blotch with needle and thread from A to B.

ASSEMBLING Cover the bent top of stem wire with d/s tape. Press on and bind 10 stamens, followed by the 5 petals which should not overlap when they are spread out.
Add leaves as for "Doris".

PATTERN 5 CARNATION and PINKS

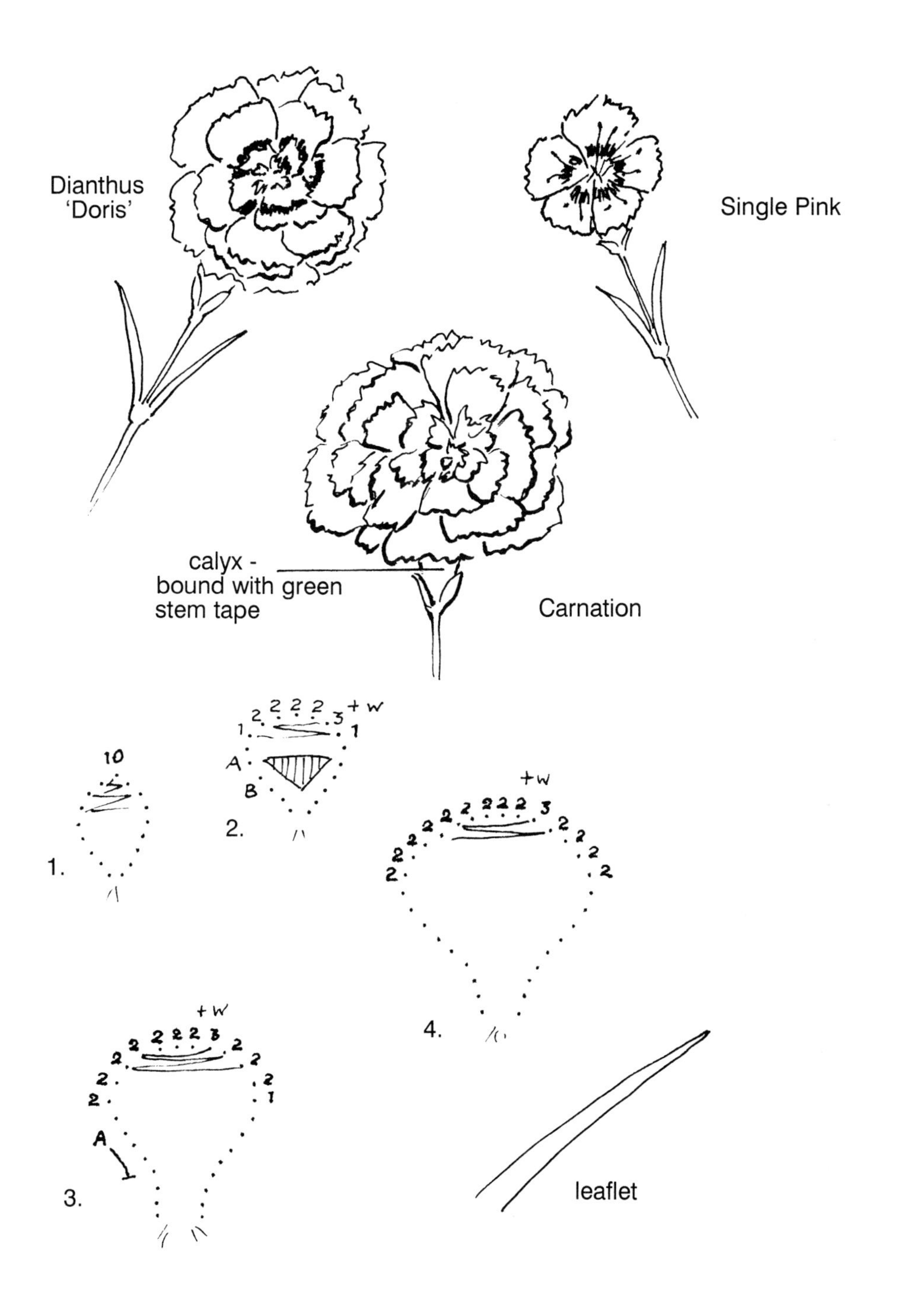

PATTERN 6

KAFFIR LILY - Schizostylus
Sylko 10 prs Gladiole Red, 5prs Orange Lily
fine wire, gauge 38
green stem wire
green stem tape
double- sided sticky tape
3 long red stamens
3 long red styles (beheaded stamens) - colour stems with a red felt-tip pen.
Pearl stamens can be used if you are not fussy as to accuracy.

FLOWER PETALS B/T 1-11 15prs and wire

Hang 10 prs open round the top pin, mixing the colours.
Weave in the wire and work the petal in cloth st, adding prs as indicated.
Edge st is cloth st and 2 twists.
Make a central ladder by twisting the worker pr, increasing from 1 to 3 twists then reducing as the petal narrows. Lay back prs until 8 remain. Bow off.
Make 6

HALF-OPEN FLOWERS are made in the same way, using the smaller pricking.
Make 6

BUDS consist of 3 bud petals stitched together and filled out with stem tape or cottonwool.

ASSEMBLING B/T 12-16

Pad the top of a short piece of stem wire with stem tape or d/s tape pressed round the hook.
Bind on 6 stamens (They should be long enough to reach the tip of the petals which are now added.) Attach 3 petals in the first ring, securing with a stitch or two, then add the other 3 in the spaces. Bind and stitch securely to keep the petals close and in order.
Cut 2 green sepals from stem tape. Wrap a small piece of d/s tape round the base of the flower and place the sepals on this, overlapping to enfold the stem. Finish off with half-width green stem tape.
Mount the smaller flowers and buds in the same way.
Cut off the heads of 3 of the stamens.

When all the flowers and buds are ready, take a full-length stem wire, turn over the end and cover it well with enough stem tape to make it look like a closed bud.
Continue binding the stem for about 15mm (1/2´´), then add the next size bud. Incorporate the graduated flowers at 25mm (1´´) intervals.

LEAVES Use the sketch opposite as a rough guide to cut and shape 2 or 3 leaves from florist's ribbon. Mount them at the base of the flower stem or on a separate piece of wire.

PATTERN 6 KAFFIR LILY

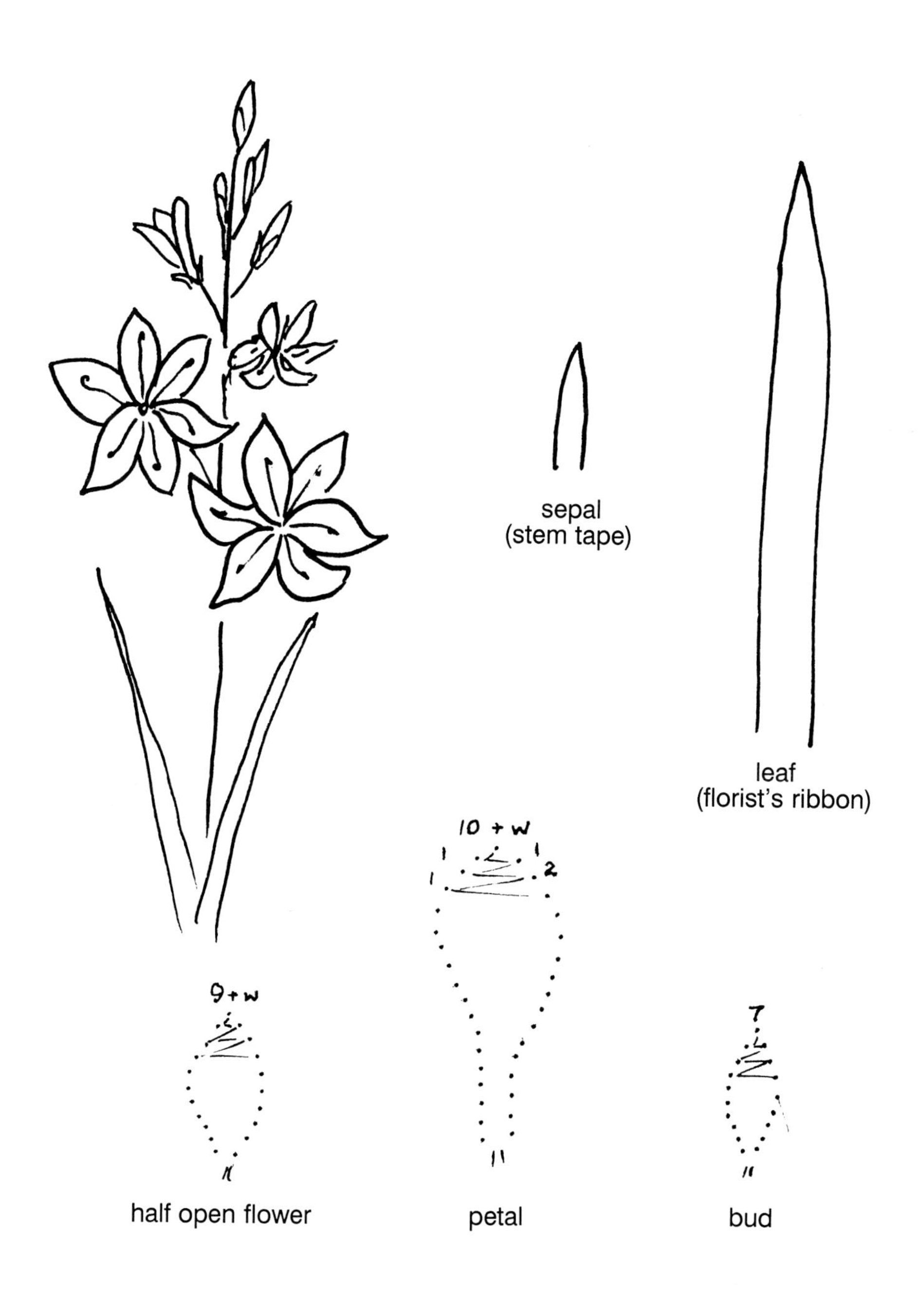

PATTERN 7

FUCHSIA - 'Mrs Popple'
Sylko 18 prs Turkey Red and Ruby, about equal numbers for outer sepals
23 prs - mostly Violet (13), Ruby (6), Royal Blue (4) for inner petals.
1 pr fine wire
stem wire, gauge 22
brown stem tape
double-sided sticky tape
9 red stamens
bought silk leaves, or made in lace - 21 prs Light and Dark Olive
(see LEAVES, page 11)

Basic Techniques 1-11

RED OUTER SEPALS 18prs, 1 pr wire

Around the top pin hang **6 Turkey Red and 4 Ruby prs**, using the Turkey Red as workers.
Twist all twice, weave wire through. Vary the position of the two colours in each sepal - this will give the highlights.
Edge st is cloth st and 2 twists.
Add 4 more prs of each colour as indicated. At x introduce ladders (see pattern 6).
Start laying back prs as the sepal narrows until 8 prs are left at the waist.
Continue to the end.
Make 4. Sew them together from waist to bottom to form a tube.

PURPLE INNER PETALS 23 prs and wire - 13 Violet, 6 Ruby, 4 Royal Blue.
Hang 2 prs round each of the 4 top pins, (alternating the colours of the single threads), and 3 prs on the next RH pin, using 2 full Violet bobbins from this pin as the worker pr. Twist all twice.
Weave the wire through all except the worker pr and tie single knots in the passives to enclose the wire and keep it close to the top edge. Take the worker through in cloth st, bringing the other wire down at the end of the row. Continue in cloth st, adding double prs at each side up to 23 prs.
Start reducing at a), mainly the blue and violet, leaving about 10 red prs at the end. Do not cut off the wire immediately, but after bowing off pull the ends **very gently** to incurve the top of the petal.
Make 4.

MEDIUM BUD 11 prs and fine wire
Use 5 Ruby and 6 Turkey Red, including the worker, all of them round the top pin.
Follow the instructions for the red sepals but sew to within 3 or 4 rows of the tips.
These are turned back as though the flower is just opening.
Make 4.

SMALL BUD 9 prs and wire.
4 Ruby and 5 Turkey Red round top pin.
Work 4 petals, bow off, cut off wire and sew all seams except the last.
Cont'd on page 32

PATTERN 7 FUCHSIA

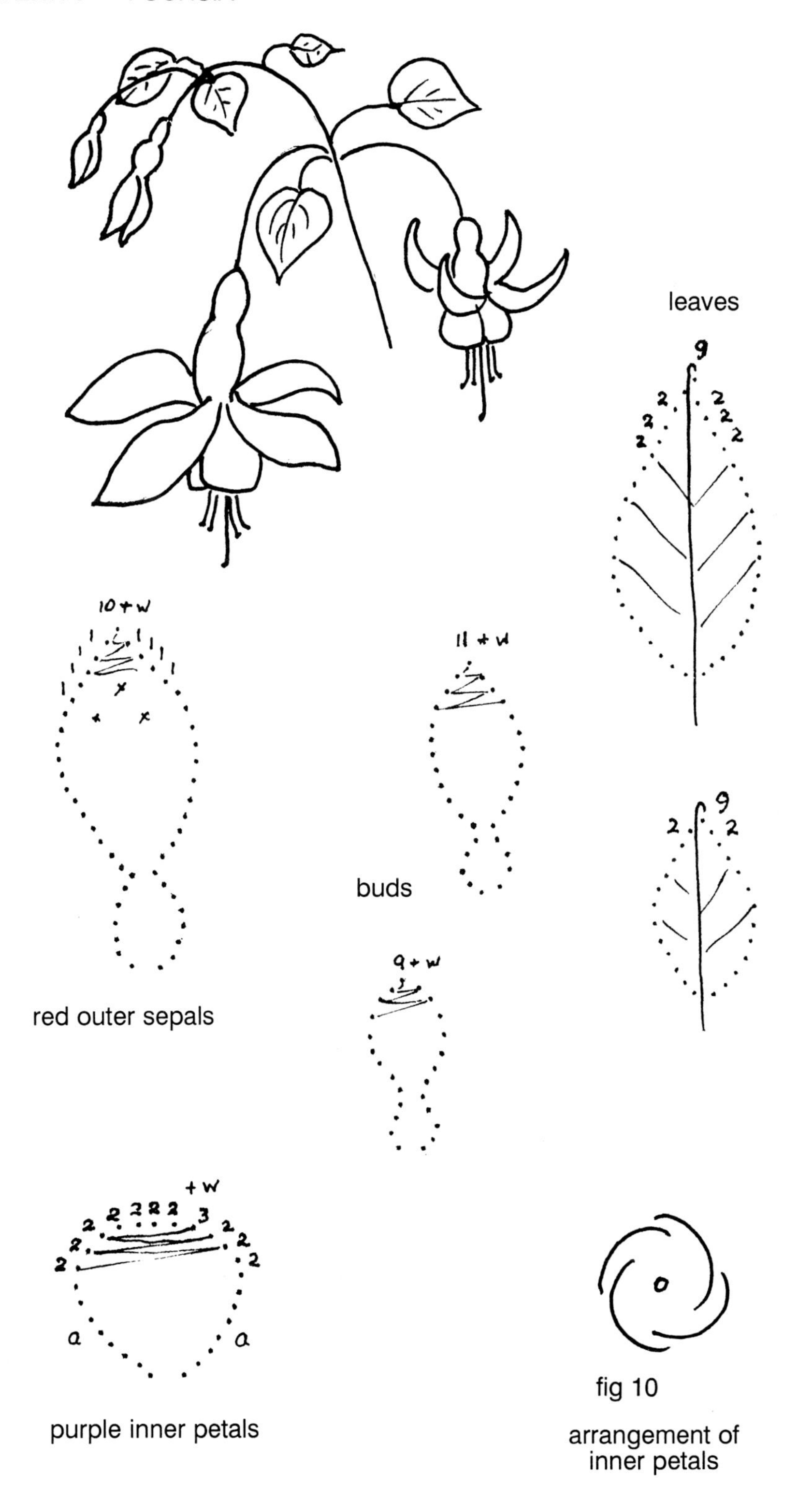

fig 10

arrangement of inner petals

PATTERN 8

IRIS

This pattern represents the various dainty bulbous types - Dutch, English, Spanish and the early Reticulata.

Sylko, 23 prs altogether - Light Lilac, Violet, Royal Blue, and a good purple (Ultramarine 529) or other Iris colours
1 pr fine wire, gauge 38
2 prs yellow embroidery thread
2 prs thicker embroidery thread in orange

double-sided sticky tape
green stem tape
green stem wire, gauge 19 or 22
florist's ribbon for leaves
3 stamens

STANDARD PETALS B/T 1-11. 15 prs - 9 Purple and 6 Royal Blue, plus wire.
Hang 9 purple and 2 blue round the top pin, alternating the colours but having 2 fully wound purple bobbins on RH side. Twist all twice, weave wire through.
Edge st is cloth st and 2 twists. Work in cloth st. adding 2 more blue prs each side.
Introduce 3 single-twist ladders with 3 passives between them (see Pattern 5, page 23).
Reduce these where the petal narrows and start laying back prs until 10 remain.
Finish petal and bow off.
Make 3.

FALL PETALS 21 prs altogether plus wire - 5 purple, 4 blue, 8 violet, 2 yellow and 2 orange.
Hang 5 purple, 4 blue and 2 violet prs alternating round the top pin, with **2 full purple bobbins** on R for the workers. Weave wire through. Work in cloth st, adding 3 more violet prs on each side (17 prs of bobbins and wire). When the centre pinhole is reached hang in 2 yellow prs, cloth st through these and on to the end. Work another plain row. In the next row hang in the thicker orange prs open round the lower centre pin, between the yellow prs. The next step is important, as if these are not anchored properly you may find the chain unravels itself - most disconcerting when you are halfway down the petal! So... twist the 2 LH threads R over L and make a halfstitch with the 2 prs. Cloth st through them to the end of the row.

Now start the **Russian Chain stitch honey guide** (*fig 11b,* opposite). Cloth st to the orange prs, twist these in opposite directions - L to L, R to R. Lift the 2 new centre **threads** up and pass the purple workers under these. Lay them back in the same place. Keep a good tension on the workers so there is no gap in the middle of the chain. Continue cloth st to the end of the row and repeat the process in each row (leaving out blue and purple towards the end of the petal). The effect is a raised chain in orange, flanked by a double yellow line simulating the honey guides .... at least it was before I made a mistake in the yellow cloth st and found I had twisted a passive pr. Now it appeared much more realistic as a jagged yellow line, so I suggest you twist the yellow passives at intervals. Many new inventions and recipes occur by accident so don't be afraid to experiment!
Make 3.

PATTERN 8 IRIS

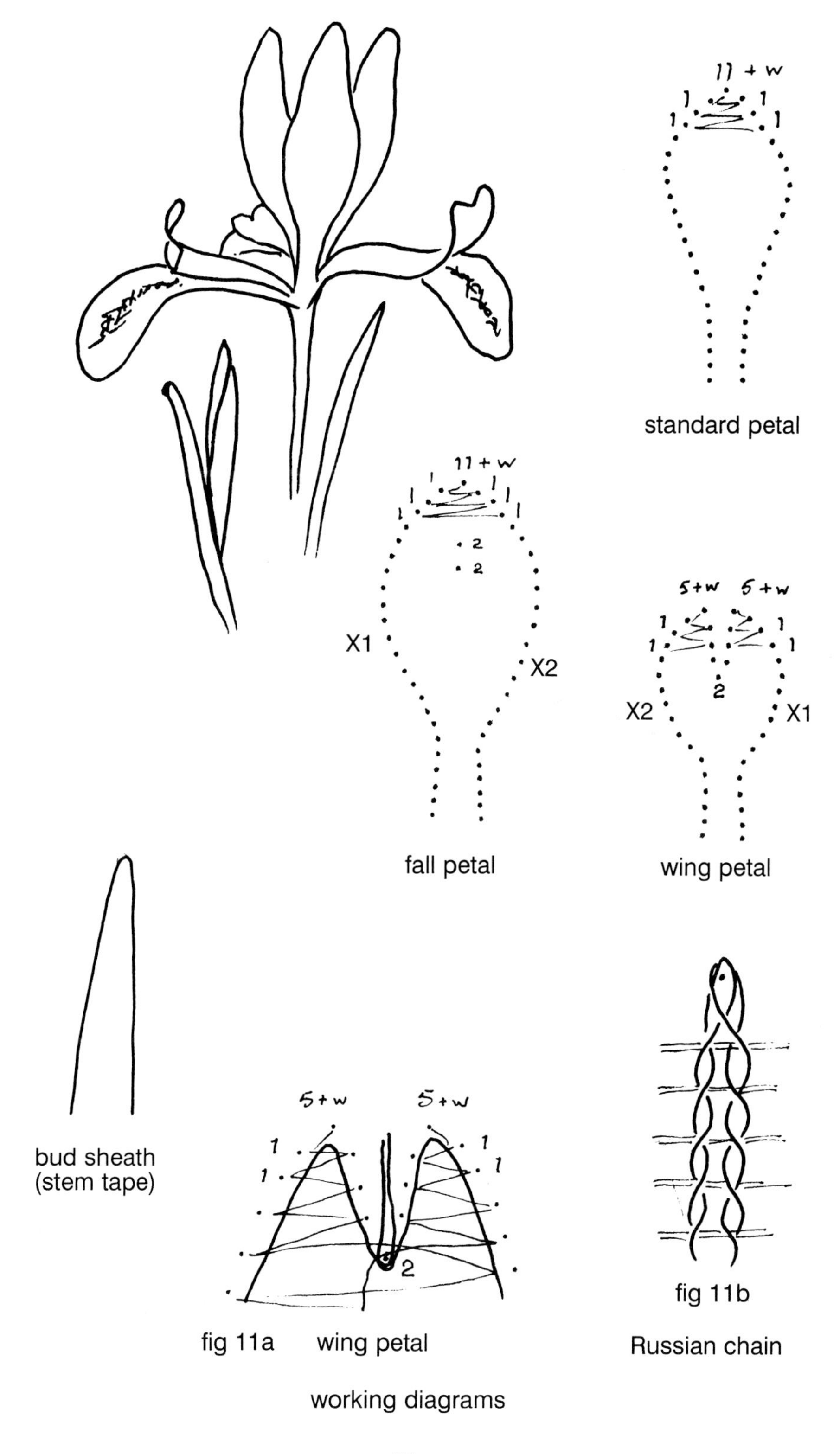

working diagrams

WINGED PETAL (*Fig 11a,* page 31) 16 prs and 2 prs wire
Start with 3 prs lilac and 2 prs violet on each of the top pins, with lilac workers on the inside.
The wire on the L point works to the R as usual, but that on the R is reversed - weaving from R to L where the worker is waiting.
Cloth st each side, adding 2 purple prs at the outer edges, until the centre pin is reached.
Cloth st the 2 worker prs together, put up the centre pin and hang 2 new purple prs **in order** over it. Continue the row with the LH worker - the RH one drops down to become a passive alongside the new purple prs. Tie the centre wires in a single knot and lay them back to be cut off later. Start to reduce at x-x, leaving out the pale colours. Make 3.

BUD Make 3 standard petals

ASSEMBLING
Match and stitch the top winged petal to the fall petal (x_1-x_1, x_2-x_2 to base) to form a tube. Place a stamen between the two (anchored with a stitch) to protrude slightly when the wings are bent back.
Bend the fall petals downwards.
Fasten standard petals to the top of a padded stem wire, to stand upright, then arrange the fall petals in the spaces. Trim the ends to 15mm (1/2´´).

Pad another stem wire for about 2.5cm (1´´). Fold the bud petals round this and stitch in place. Cut 2 full-width pieces of stem tape and place them overlapping round the bud (d/s tape helps here). Bind from halfway down the bud, then down the stem.

Some types of iris buds arise on the main flower stem, in which case place the stem of the bud against the flower stem and bind both together to the end of the flower stem.

LEAVES can be shaped from florist's ribbon as in the Kaffir Lily, pattern 6.

FUCHSIA (continued from page 28)
Prepare a full-length stem wire, padding the hooked end with a small piece of cottonwool bound on with brown stem tape. Place this onto the wrong side of the petals and sew up the last seam. Trim the ends.
This long wire will have the rest of the leaves and flowers attached to it.

ASSEMBLING B/T 12-16

Fasten 8 stamens and a much longer one round the hooked end of a 75mm (3´´) stem wire.
Over these arrange the inner petals as in the diagram (*fig 10,* page 29), making sure the wrong side is inside so the trimmed ends are hidden.
Bind the loose ends onto the wire with thread or a small piece of stem tape so that the stem can be passed easily down into the tube at the base of the red sepals. Trim all ends to 15mm (1/2´´), not graduated, as this will form the bulge below the sepal tube. Mount the rest of the buds and flowers on the first bud stem and bind all together.

LEAVES - see page 12. Use the fuchsia leaf pricking and instructions for Pinnate leaves.
Finish off as B/T 16, arranging buds, leaves and flowers as in illustration.

PATTERNS 1, 2, 3, 4, and 7

PATTERNS

5b	Pink 'Doris'	Page 24	10	Sweet Pea	Page 36
5c	Single Pink	Page 24	14b	Spring Snowflake	Page 46
6	Kaffir lily	Page 26	14c	Summer Snowflake	Page 46
7	Fuchsia	Page 28	19	Bell shapes	Page 52
8	Iris	Page 30	20	Berries	Page 52
9	Freesia	Page 33	7	Leaf	Page 11,13 and with patterns

Orange Tip
Common Blue
Painted Lady
Purple Emperor

PATTERN 9

FREESIA
As this is such a delicate flower it calls for different treatment - a finer thread, more ladders and a **'straight' edge.**

14 prs DMC Broder machine 50 or Madeira cotona 50
in 2 toning shades
1 pr fine wire
green stem wire
green stem tape
double-sided sticky tape
1 long stamen on its own green stem (*fig 12*, page 35, also see end)
3 stamen stems stained the colour of the flower (with felt-tip pen).

Variegated thread is useful in these petals but it is important to wind bobbins so that a good span of the darker colour is in use on the 6 full worker bobbins while their partners form the dark centre.

Straight edge - cloth st as far as but not through the last pr, twist worker pr once, pin up, cloth st and 1 twist with the edge pr which now becomes the new worker, leaving the previous worker to rest at the side. It is customary to have 2 or 3 twists on this type of edge stitch, which gives a more defined edge line, but one twist leaves a narrower gap, please yourself.

PETAL 14 prs plus wire
Arrange the bobbins open round the pin so that you have -
4 full **bobbins** on R
2 full **bobbins** on L
their knotted or sparse partner threads hanging in between
6 more prs as passives
2 darker prs in the centre.

Twist all twice. Starting at the second pr on L, weave through all except the 2 end prs at R.
Cloth st these together, twist once, then use the inner pr as workers to cloth st across the row to L, starting with the wire and its partner. Before the last pr, bring round and down the other wire to partner the odd coloured thread. Cloth st through this pr pin up between these, twist worker and cloth st with the outside edge pr. Use the inner pr as the new worker.

Pairs to be added are taken up over the worker **after the pin is set but before the edge st is worked**, brought down as usual inside the wire, **then the edge st is made up** (beware - this is so easy to forget!) and the resting worker brought into use (B/T5 *fig 4c*, page 8). There should now be 14 prs plus wire on the pillow.

If, because of your particular working tension, the passives seem to pull away from the edge pr, work the edge stitch and back through the wire and its partner, then tie the workers once (half a reef). Another tip for good tension - at the completion of each row stretch out the two outside prs (workers and resting workers).

Now start lightening the fabric with **cloth st and twist** across the row to the end wire. At the widest part of the petal use 2 twists for 4 or 5 rows, to spread the passives across the row. As the petal narrows change back to plain cloth st, laying back several threads in each row until 10 prs remain, then halfway down the tube reduce to 8 and work ordinary edges (cloth st, 2 twists, cloth st). Bow off and trim laid back prs.

Make 6 petals for each flower, 3 for the half-open flower, and 2 or 3 in plain cloth st without wire for tight buds.

ASSEMBLING Fasten the 3 stamen stalks round the long stamen head or padded wire (*fig 12* opposite).
With self-coloured thread bind 3 petals round this so that the bottoms are level. The thick stamen or padded wire will support the petal tube. Stitch the petal edges together to form a tube, add the other petals in the spaces and also stitch these up to where the petals widen. Fan out the tops.
Make graded buds in the same way, using only the 3 inner petals and stitching all seams. The long stamen can be padded out further with cottonwool to retain the full bud shape.
For sepals use a small piece of full-width stem tape, trimmed as the template. Arrange it round the base of the flower - a tiny piece of d/s tape ensures that it stays in place while you bind the bottom of the flower and stem in the usual way with half-width stem tape. Mount the buds in the same way.

When all the flowers and buds are fixed on their stems take a full-length stem wire, turn over the tip and bind it with enough stem tape to make it look like a closed bud. Continue binding the stem for 15mm (1/2´´) then add another bud, leaving about the same length of stem showing. Carry on binding the main stem, adding in the buds and flowers, all facing upwards.
Bind the rest of the stem and bend it into its natural shape.

STAMENS It is not always possible to buy the exact type of stamen you want. In this flower the wire itself can be padded out well below the tip to help fill out the petal tube.
Another way of getting round it is to use **petal paste**, obtainable from Sugarcraft shops, or beg a small lump if you are fortunate enough to have a Sugarcraft friend! Dampen the bound wire and mould a small piece of the well-kneaded yellow paste around it into the required shape. If there is some paste left over you can experiment with it by pressing out small pea-sized lumps very thinly into the shape of the Patio Rose pattern no. 1. Press these petals round the top of the wire as in the Assembling Instructions for the rose. Stand the wired flowers and stamens upright to dry out.
You are now into another fascinating Flower hobby!

PATTERN 9 FREESIA

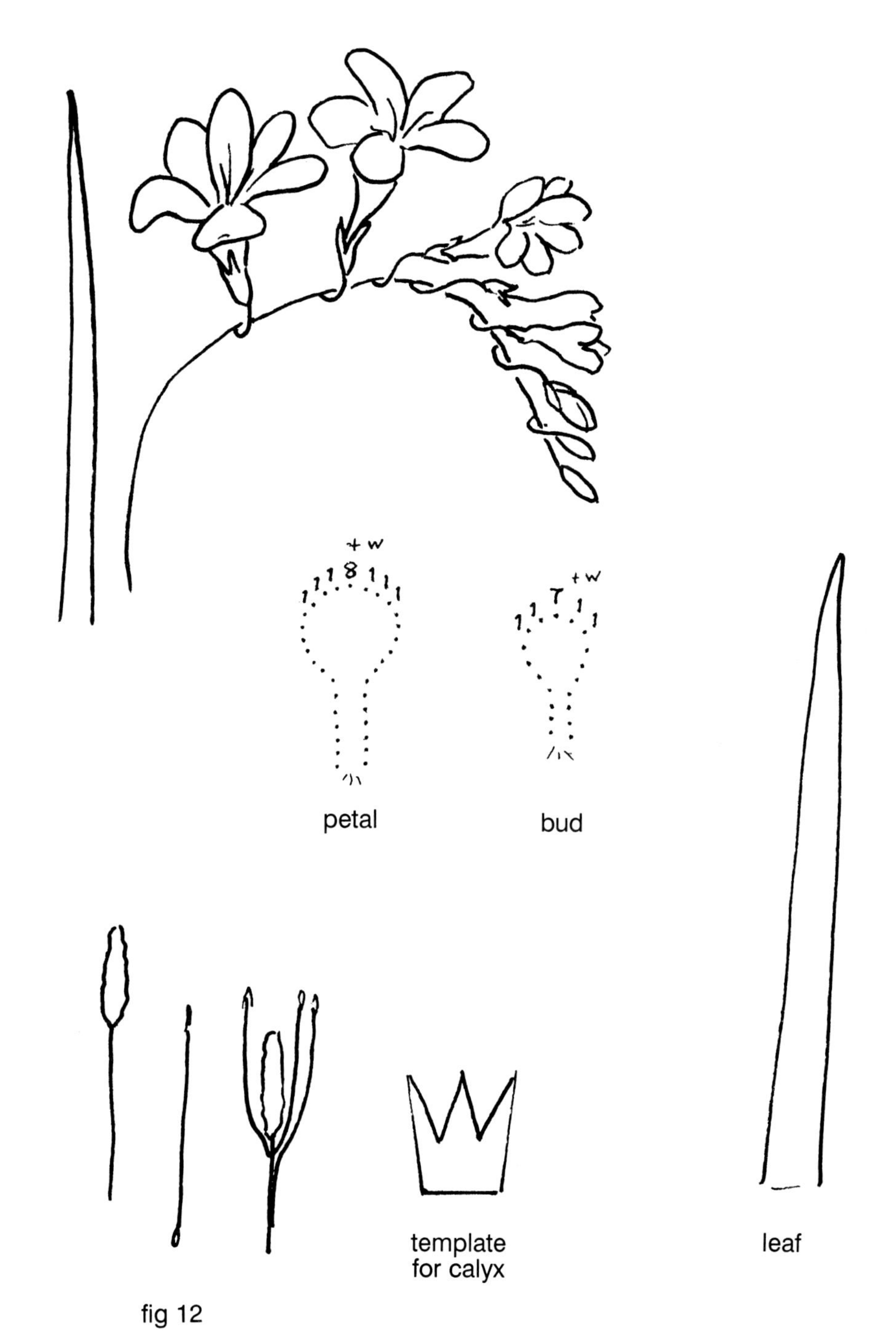

fig 12

PATTERN 10

SWEET PEA - Lathyrus odorata
27 prs Sylko in toning sweet pea colours

fine lacquered wire, pink
green plasticised stem wire
green stem tape
double-sided sticky tape
green florist's ribbon

A large pillow is essential for this pattern

LARGE PETAL B/T 1-16 27 prs plus wire
Hang 2 prs round each of the 6 top pins as well as 3 prs on the 7th, making sure there is **a full bobbin** on the extreme R for the worker (weaver).

Twist all twice, weave wire through.
Work the petal in half-stitch, with **edges in cloth st, 2 twists on worker, pin up, cloth st and 1 twist on worker.** The full bobbin will then be in position to lead the half-stitch back across the row.
Add 2 prs on each row, as shown, bringing them down inside the wire, until all 28 prs are in use (B/T 5, *fig 4b*). Swing the bobbins well across the pillow to ensure an even tension.
Juggle with colours to achieve shaded effects.
Bow off in 2 bunches. **Be sure to adjust knots close to the 'sparse' bobbin and at least 5 cm (2´´) below the bottom of the pattern.**
Make 2, using the 2nd one reversed when assembling so that the straight edges come together and are stitched to make one large petal.

MEDIUM PETAL 24 prs and wire
Work as above. Make 2

SMALL PETAL (KEEL) 14 prs plus wire
Hang 10 prs open round the top pin, with 2 full bobbins at R. Twist all twice and weave wire through (B/T 4). Half-stitch throughout as above, adding prs at each side up to the full total.
Bind in one bunch, bow off and trim to 2.5cm (1´´). Make 1.

ASSEMBLING Cut the calyx in green florist's ribbon, using the template.
Sew the sides of the small petal together to form the keel, twisting the spare threads up inside to pad it out. Push a hooked stem wire into this and fasten securely (this mounted petal may be used on its own for a bud, surrounded by a calyx). Place the overlapping medium petals over the folded side of the bud like a saddle. Stitch in place, then stitch the 2 large petals together near the inner edge and place at the back in the same way. Fasten securely and trim ends to 10mm (about 1/2´´). Bind the flower base and ends with d/s tape, press the calyx round this and again bind with d/s tape. The green stem tape can now be applied in the usual way.
Mount 2 or 3 flowers and buds on one main stem.

PATTERN 10 SWEET PEA

27 + w

outer edge

h.st

large petal - make 2

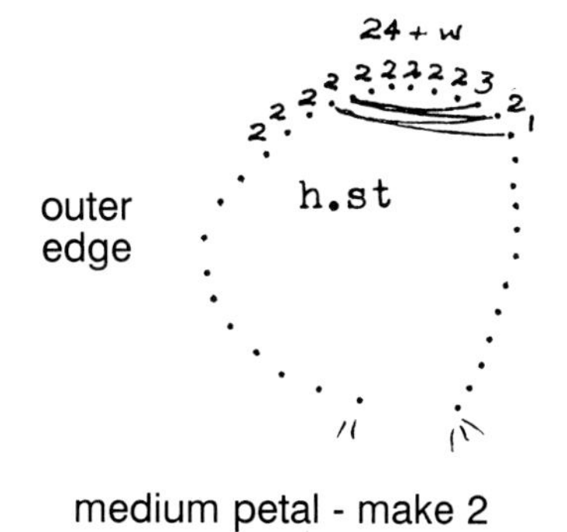

medium petal - make 2

small petal - make 1

calyx template (florist's ribbon)

PATTERN 11

CYCLAMEN PERSICUM - winter flowering house plant
Sylko 19 prs cyclamen colours - 7 prs Pale Rose,
6 prs White and 6 prs Cerise
or 13 prs Geranium and 6 prs Cerise
1 pr fine wire
green plasticised stem wire gauge 22
brown stem tape
double-sided sticky tape
blue-green florist's ribbon, latex or silk leaves, cut to shape
6 beheaded stamens

PETAL B/T1-11 19 prs plus wire
Hang 5 white prs and 4 pale pink prs open round the top pin, using 2 full white bobbins for the workers. Keep the pink prs towards the edges but alternate some to graduate the shading.
Twist all twice, weave the wire through.
Edge st is cloth st and 2 twists.
Work in cloth st, adding a pink pr at each end of the next row and white prs in the following row. Continue as far as x - x, where the cerise colour is introduced. Hang 5 prs over the centre pins, more or less alternating with several pale colours. Cloth st through these, make up the edge st, then hang a dark pr over the pin and use this as the worker. In the next 3 rows lay back all the pale colours except the edge passives, leaving 8 prs to finish the petal.
Bow off and trim the laid back prs close to the work.
Make 5.

BUD Use a total of 12 prs, with a pink pr on each outer edge (with the pink wire this means 3 darker threads each side). Graduate the white prs to the centre. There is no dark patch at the bottom.
Make 3.

ASSEMBLING Sew the petals together from just below the start of the dark threads to form a short narrow tube. Fasten 5 short and 1 long beheaded stamen stems to the top of the padded stem wire and thread this carefully, stem first, through the flower tube so that the stamens are level with the start of the dark section (*fig 13* opposite). Trim and secure the loose threads to the stem, then add the calyx, bind and finish off with brown stem tape. Bend back the petals so that the dark area is showing and give them a slight twist. Bend over the stem into its natural shape.

BUD Pad out the top of a hooked stem wire with brown stem tape. Overlap the bud petals, secure them with a stitch or two at the bottom, then fold them in a spiral round the padded stem. Add the calyx, bind with brown stem tape and bend the stem head right over.

LEAVES These can be made from florist's ribbon, latex or from bought silk leaves, cut to shape and marked.

PATTERN 11 CYCLAMEN PERSICUM

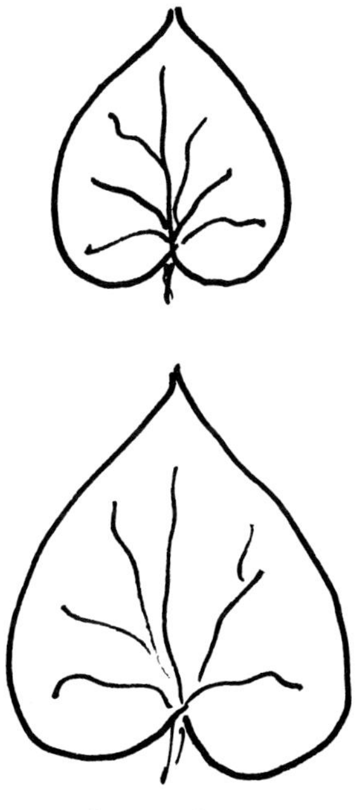

leaves in florist's ribbon or latex

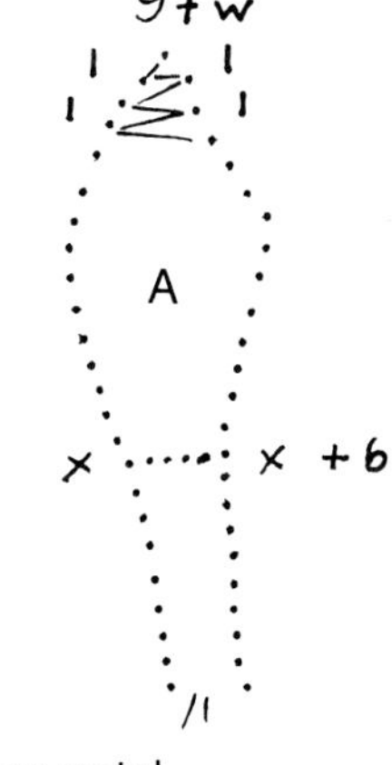

flower petal

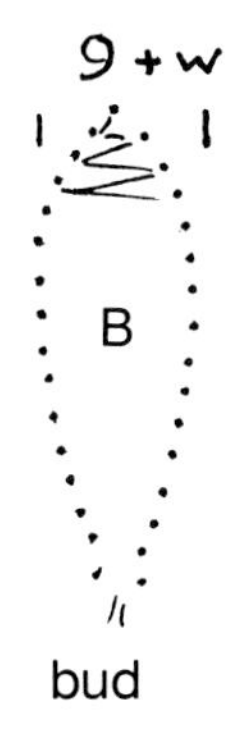

bud

brown calyx (stem tape)

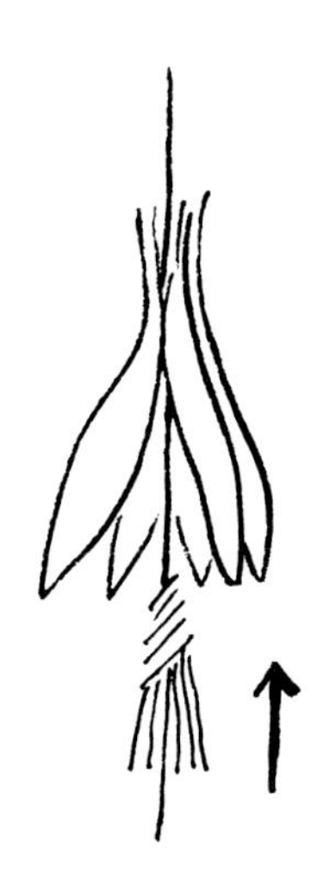

fig 13

PATTERN 12

ANEMONE de CAEN - wind flower
21 prs Sylko or DMC 30 in anemone colours
15 prs extra for bi-coloured flowers
1 pr fine wire
numerous black stamens
2.5 cm (1´´) square piece of black velvet
green stem wire, gauge 22
green stem tape
double-sided tape
bought silk leaves as no.6 on page 13, cut to shape for bracts.

A variety of colours and stitches can be used to make a natural bunch of anemones, using the basic pattern. Make about 7 petals for each flower.
B/T 1-11

FLOWER 1 Basic pattern. Plain cloth stitch. **Edge st cloth st and 2 twists.** Start with 11 coloured prs round the top pin. Twist all twice, weave the wire through and work in cloth st, adding prs at each end until all 21 prs are in. Reduce to about 10 as the petal narrows.

FLOWER 2 Half-stitch. Edge st is cloth st and 2 twists, pin up, followed by cloth st and 1 twist on the worker. Make sure the full bobbin is the leader and is now in position to lead in half-st back across the row. Added prs must be brought down inside the wire (B/T 5, *fig 4b,* page 8).

FLOWER 3 Cloth st with ladders and straight edge
At L edge make sure there are 2 full bobbins and at R edge 4 full bobbins. After adding the wire, cloth st the 2 RH prs and use the inner pr to work across the row in cloth st. Before working the last stitch put up the pin, add new prs, (*fig 4c,* page 8), cloth st and 2 twists with the outer pr, and return with the inner pr. The outer pr is now the “resting worker”. The wire is third from the edge.
Repeat this until all prs are in. Start ladders as indicated on the pricking and reduce prs where the petal narrows.

FLOWER 4 Two colours. 21 prs red (or purple) 15 prs white, 1 pr wire. Many deep-coloured anemones have a white centre. Work in cloth st (Basic pattern, Flower 1) as far as **A**. Start adding 14 white prs alternately across the row (hanging from a hat-pin above the work, with all the other pins pushed down), leaving the wire and 7 red **threads** each side. Work 2 rows to compress the coloured threads, then carefully lift the hat-pin and lodge it horizontally behind the last pin on each side (*fig 14b* opposite). Gently ease the white loops down. This allows normal tension on the passives without risking gaps in the cloth. Lay all the coloured prs to the back except for the edge prs. Now introduce the last white pr as the new worker, hanging it over the end pin.
Gradually reduce the passives to about 10 prs, starting with the coloured bands at the sides.
Bow off and trim the coloured laid-back threads close to the work.

ASSEMBLING B/T 12-14 (*fig 14a* opposite)
With small pliers, form the top of the stem wire into a small ball and cover

this with the piece of black velvet, **fastening it securely** with needle and thread. Around this bind plenty of black stamens, using a small piece of d/s tape, followed by the petals. Trim ends and finish as B/T 12-16, incorporating a jagged silk leaf below the flower for the bracts. No other leaves are needed.

PATTERN 12 ANEMONE de CAEN

1 2 4 3

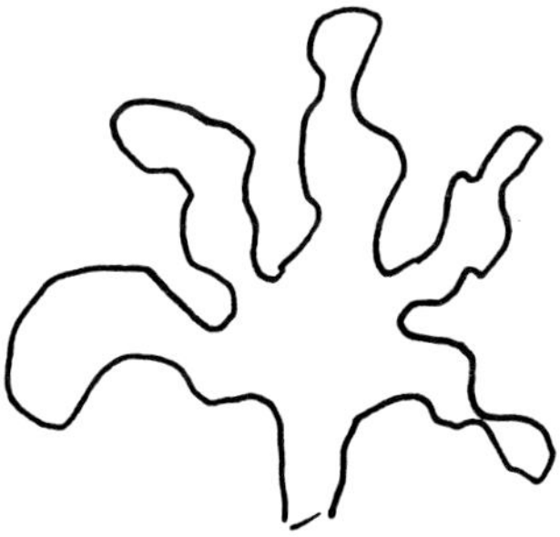

bract cut from
a bought silk leaf

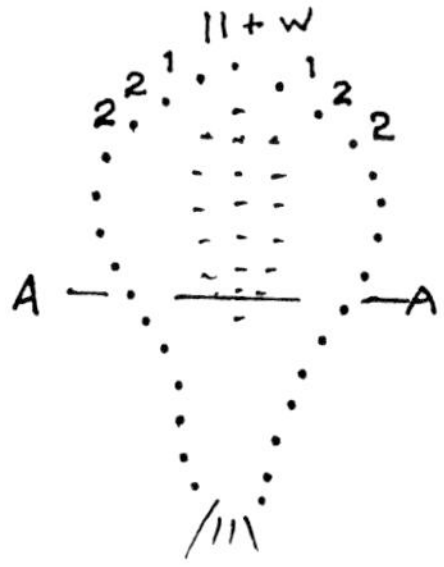

11 + w
2 2 1 1 2 2
A A

support pin

fig 14a

A A

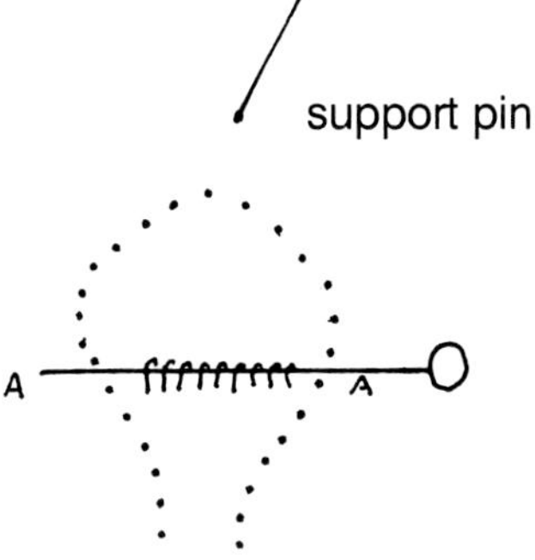

fig 14b

PATTERN 13

GENTIAN
There are many varieties of gentian, flowering from early spring till autumn, and in different shades of blue - from purple to petrol blue. Specialists also have white, pink and yellow but the most well-known is Gentian acaulis. The following colours will achieve a good result, adding lime green for the honey guides.

19 prs Sylko - 9 Radiant Blue, 6 Royal Blue and 4 Spectrum Violet mixed
3 prs Lime Green
1 pr fine wire
double-sided sticky tape
green plasticised stem wire
green stem tape
green florist's ribbon
several yellow stamens

PETALS 22 prs plus wire
Hang 9 prs mixed colours open round the top pin, with 2 full Royal Blue bobbins as workers on R. Twist all twice, weave wire through and work 5 rows cloth st, adding prs on each side (see working diagram *fig 15a* opposite). **Edge st is cloth st and 2 twists.**
Row 6 Take the worker as far as but not through the wire and partner. Put up a pin and hang 2 prs over this **in order** so that they hang in their original pairs (*fig 15b* opposite).
On the next pin to R hang 3 more prs of mixed bobbins, again in order. Weave the waiting wire through the new prs and follow with the worker. Put up the edge pin, add 1 more pr over the worker and cloth st back to the L edge.
On the next row work to the centre pinhole (about 7 stitches) then hang in 1 Lime Green pr. Two rows later hang in another green pr on each side of it. Leave these 3 pins in. Continue in cloth st.
Where the petal narrows start laying back blue prs until there are only 3 prs on each side of the green (10 altogether). Complete the petal and bow off. Make 5.

BUD Make 2 petals

ASSEMBLING Sew the petals together from A downwards to form a tube. Pad the top of a hooked stem wire with cottonwool and cover it with green stem tape. Fasten several stamens to this and thread, stem first, down through the petal tube, which is then fastened securely (*fig 13*, page 39). Cut the calyx from full-width stem tape, using the template. Wrap a small piece of d/sided tape round the base of the flower and press the calyx onto this before binding with half-width stem tape. Finish the stem to the base.

BUD - sew petals together, pad wire with cottonwool, push into the petal tube, add calyx and bind with stem tape.

LEAVES can be shaped from florist's ribbon and the veins indented with a blunt instrument (see page 12)

PATTERN 13 GENTIAN

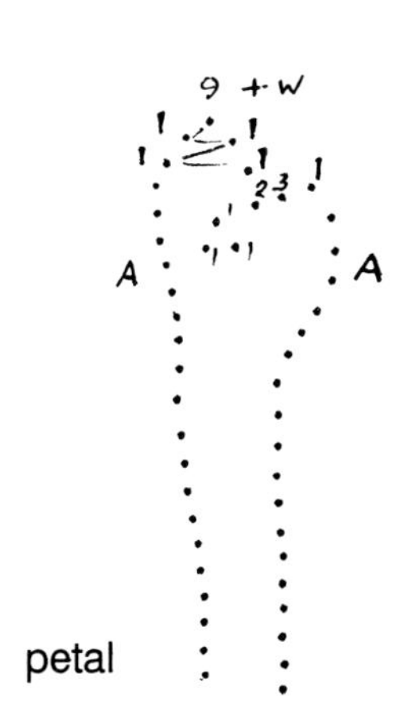

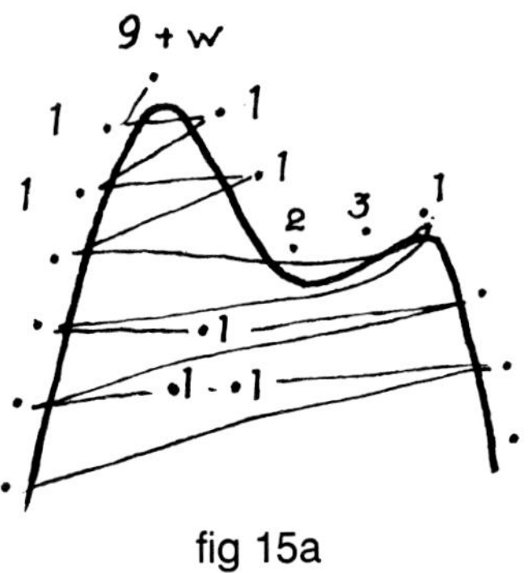

fig 15a

working diagram

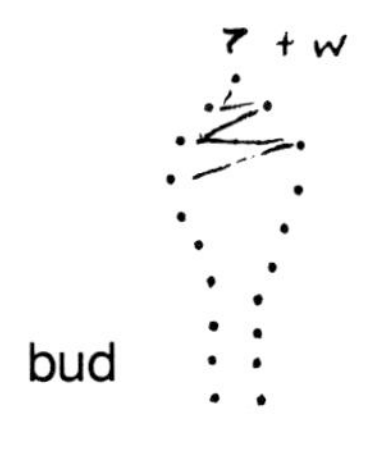

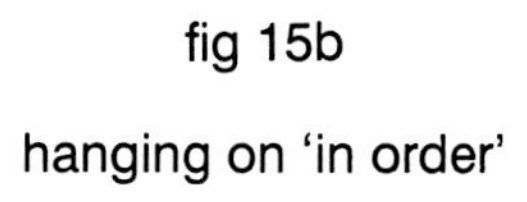

fig 15b

hanging on 'in order'

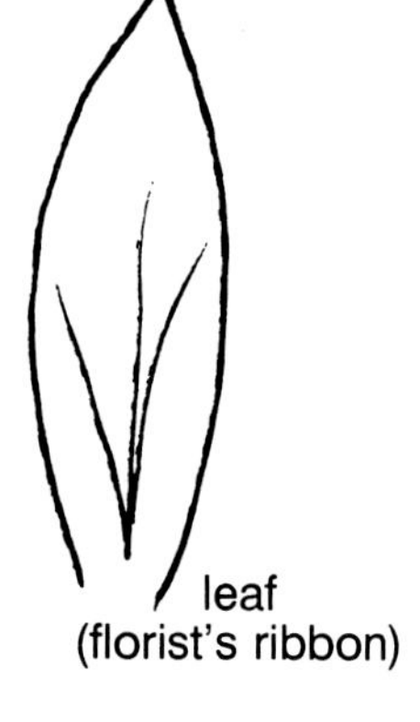

leaf
(florist's ribbon)

calyx template
(stem tape)

PATTERN 14

SPARKLING DOUBLE SNOWDROP and SNOW FLAKES
A snowdrop is not just a snowdrop. There are dozens of varieties and some specialists charge pounds for a single bulb! The ones we all know are the single and double common snowdrop, Galanthus nivalis; others are distinguished by the form, number and markings of the inner petals, the arrangement and form of leaves, the flower stem and spathe behind the flower. It is worthwhile examining an established patch to see the different markings that have evolved. The slightly later and taller 'spring' and 'summer' snowflake is often mistaken for a snowdrop, but although of the same family, its proper name is Leucojum. Its petals are all the same length in a bell shape and there are often 2 or more flower heads to a stem.

THE SNOWDROP is worked with sparkling passives and white Sylko workers, no wire.

12 prs Madeira Metallic 40, colour 300
2 prs white Sylko
6 prs Moss Green (double threads)

green stem tape
green stem wire
double-sided sticky tape
florist's ribbon for leaves and spathe
6 short yellow stamens for the snowdrop
6 longer yellow stamens for snowflakes

OUTER PETALS pricking A B/T 1-3, 5-11. 14 prs
Hang 7 prs Metallic thread on the top pin, with 2 full bobbins of white Sylko at RH side (the sparse partners hanging somewhere in the middle). Twist all twice.
Edge st is cloth st and 2 twists.
Cloth st throughout, adding prs at each end until all are included. Reduce to 8 prs at the narrowest part. Bow off. Make 3 or more.
To form the natural shape run a fingernail down the centre of the wrong side to make a slight hollow.

INNER PETALS pricking B
12 prs white Sylko, or 10 Metallic and 2 prs Sylko
6 prs Moss Green for the horseshoe (or Willow Pattern Bridge, as it is sometimes called). Refer to *fig 16a* opposite.
Hang 2 prs on each of the top 3 pins, and 3 prs on the R of these, making sure there are 2 full bobbins at the edge for the workers.
ROW 1 Work across in cloth st, add 2 prs at L pin.
ROW 2 Cloth st across, adding 1 more pr on R pin (12 prs)
ROW 3 Cloth st 3, hang in 1 green pr over the 1st interior pin, cloth st 6, (this includes the green pr), add another green pr over the next pin, cloth st through this to the end.
ROW 4 Cloth st 5, add 1 green pr on the 2nd interior pin, cloth st 4, add another green pr, cloth st to the end.
ROW 5 Cloth st 3, lay back the 1st green pr, cloth st 3, add 1 green pr on lowest inner pin, cloth st 2, add the final green pr, cloth st 4, lay back the

outer green pr, cloth st 3. The green and white prs lie alternately (18 prs).
ROW 6 Lay back the next 2 outer green prs.
ROW 7 Lay back the last 2 green prs.

Continue without further reducing.
Of course a much easier way to indicate the green marking would be with a felt-tip pen - but not for proper lacemakers!
Make 5 or more.

ASSEMBLING B/T 12-14, 16 (no sepals)
Cut off green threads close to the work
Prepare the stem wire and bind on 6 short stamens.
Overlap the inner petals, wrong side inside, and bind well. Add the 3 outer petals and stitch together at the base to prevent them moving out of place. Add other outer petals if made. Trim, bind neatly with stem tape and incorporate a short spathe about 2.5cm (1´´) from the flower. Work in 2 leaves on opposite sides at the base of the bound stem. Finally, bend the flower head down over your finger, away from the spathe.

PATTERN 14 COMMON SNOWDROP (a)

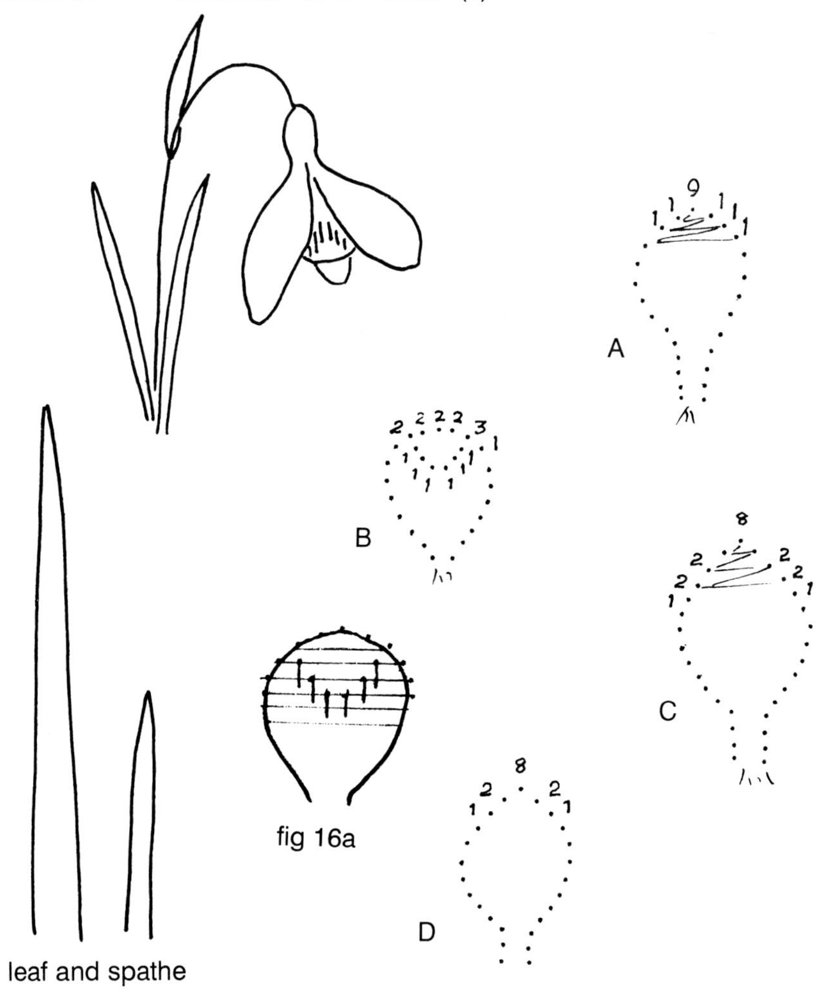

SPRING SNOWFLAKE (Leucojum vernum)

Outer petals Pricking C 18 or 19 prs white. Lime green thread for the blotch.
Start with 8 prs, cloth st throughout. No wire is necessary. Add prs as indicated, reducing to 8 towards the end. Slightly pull the edge passives to curve the petals.

Inner petals Pricking D 14 prs
Start with 8 prs on the top pin. Work as the outer petal.
Make 3

SUMMER SNOWFLAKE (Leucojum aestivum)
Pricking A 14 prs white. Lime green thread for the blotch.
Make 6 petals as Snowdrop outer petal. All petals are the same size.

ASSEMBLING First embroider a Lime Green blotch at the pointed tip of all the petals (*fig 16b* below). Bind 6 yellow stamens onto a full-length stem wire and follow with the 3 inner petals. Stitch these together to hold in place. Add the outer petals in the spaces and put a stitch in these too. Form into a bell shape with the pointed ends turning out.
For the Summer Snowflake assemble 2 more flowers on short stems. Start binding the first flower, adding the others about 2.5cm (1″) apart.
Immediately below the flowers wrap a green ribbon spathe round the stem and continue binding to the end.
Bend all the flowers over a finger to hang in line, with the spathe standing up behind.

Plain white Sylko may be substituted for the Metallic thread for any of these flowers, but the effect is not as interesting.

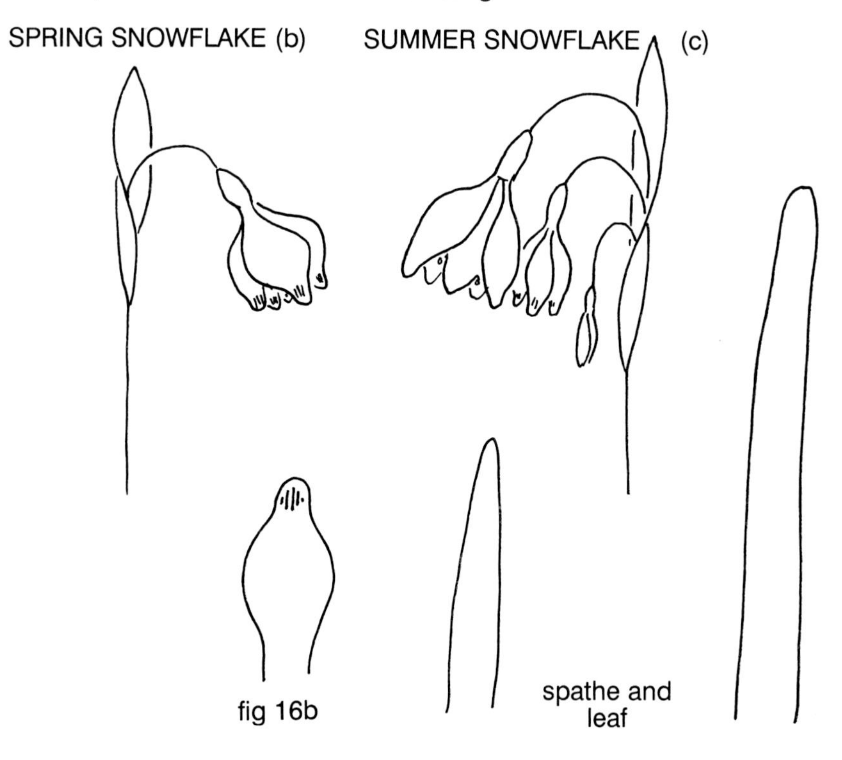

fig 16b

BRITISH WILD FLOWERS

PATTERN 15

COMMON POPPY

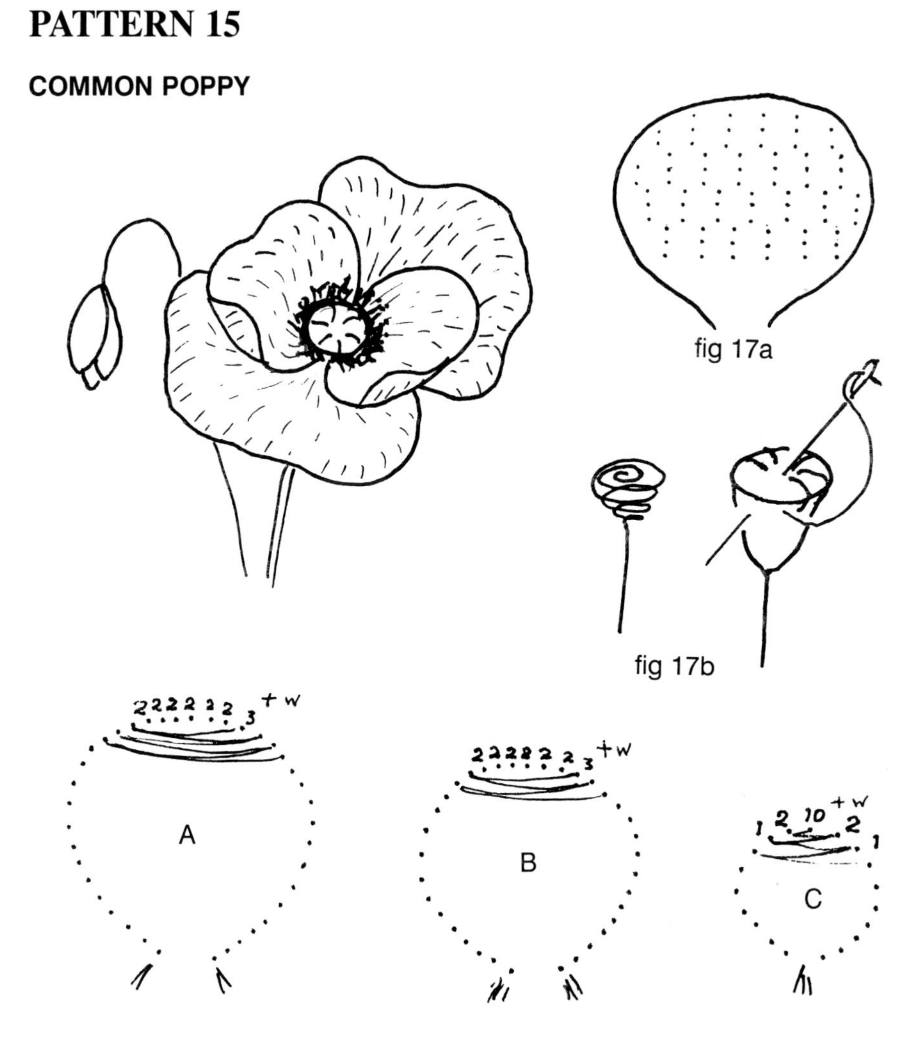

fig 17a

fig 17b

PATTERN 20 BERRIES (instructions on page 52)

PATTERN 15

COMMON POPPY

Sylko 28 prs Scarlet, Flame and Poppy mixed
16 prs Moss Green
numerous black stamens
fine wire
green stem tape
green stem wire gauge 19 or 22
double-sided sticky tape

LARGE PETAL (Pricking A) B/T 1-16
28 prs plus fine wire
Hang in as indicated, using 2 full scarlet bobbins as workers. Weave wire through but before working across the row tie each passive pr in a single knot to keep the wire close to the top edge. Add 2 prs each side until all 28 prs are in use. Work in cloth stitch with **staggered ladders** to give the crinkled silk effect - work 3 rows of ladders with 3 stitches between each, then move sideways 1 stitch and work 3 more rows, and so on to the bottom (*fig 17a* page 47). Bow off in 2 bunches.
Make 2.

SMALL PETAL (Pricking B)
24 prs plus wire
Work as above.
Make 2.

BUD (Pricking C)
16 prs plus wire
In plain cloth st make 2 red and 2 green petals

SEED CAPSULE Twist the top of a stem wire into an inverted cone, similar to the anemone centre but with the widest part at the top. Cover this with green stem tape moulded down well. Stitch lines of black thread radiating from the centre of the top as shown in *fig 17b* page 47.

ASSEMBLING Bind the stamens round the seed capsule.
Trim the loose ends of the petals and blacken them with felt-tip pen so they will merge with the stamens.
The poppy has no calyx as the seed capsule is above the petals, so a different method of assembly is called for. Lay the large petal along the top end of the stem wire, wrong side uppermost, so that the base of the petal comes to the bottom of the seed pod, the loose ends lying along the stamens.
Bind on securely and place the other large petal on the opposite side in a similar way. Put a stitch or two to fasten the petals together.
Hold the stem upright and place the small petals opposite each other where the larger petals are joined. Bind on and trim the blackened ends level with the stamens. Stroke the petals forward over the stamens - the larger petals will now be on the outside. Stitch again.

BUD Stitch the seams of the red petals together to form a bud shape, pushing the loose threads inside for padding. Over this place the green sepals, opposite each other. Put a few stitches in these too, and push the ends inside. Push the hooked end of a bound stem wire inside the bud and fasten securely. Finally, bend the stem over a finger, as in the snowdrop. The red flower bud will peep between the green sepals which in nature drop off as the flower opens.

PATTERN 16

DOG ROSE - Rosa canina
28 prs pink and white Sylko, mixed.

fine lacquered wire
green plasticised stem wire
green stem tape
double-sided sticky tape
a large pillow

Refer to Sweet Pea, Pattern 10 (Large petal), page 36, for detailed working instructions.

Make 5 petals, and 5 sepals as for Patio Rose (Pattern 1, page 14).

Stamens - make a tuft of yellow Anchor Stranded - wind a length round a finger, tie through the bunch with cotton or fine wire, snip the threads and fasten to the top of a hooked stem wire.
Assemble as B/T 10-16.

Leaves - use a spray of small bought rose leaves.

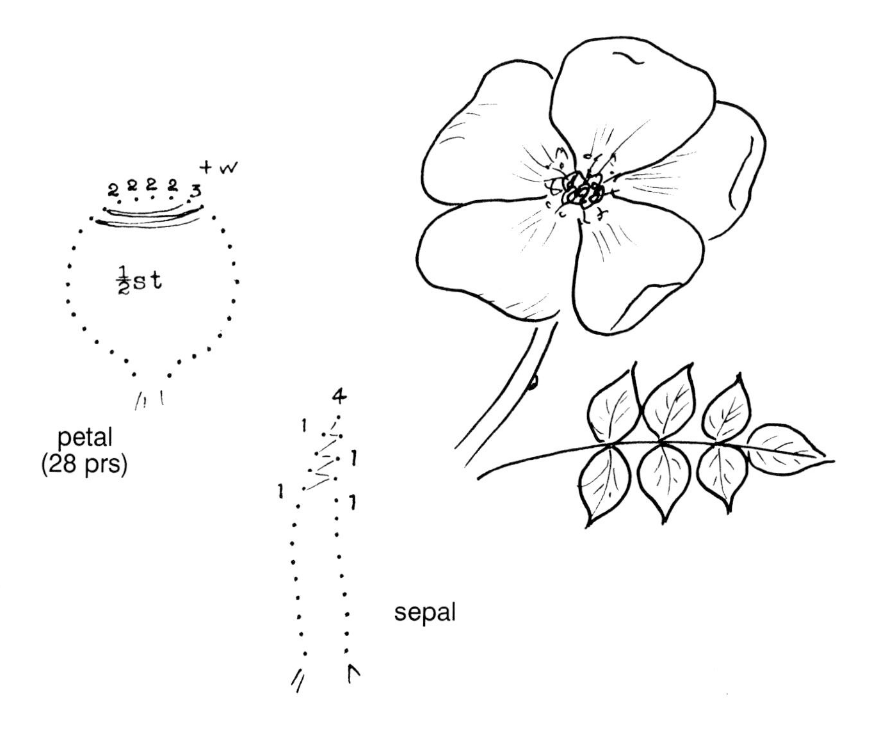

PATTERN 17

BUTTERCUP

Sylko 12 prs Buttercup Yellow
4 prs White
fine wire
green stem tape
green stem wire
double-sided sticky tape
numerous yellow stamens

PETAL Hang 2 yellow prs on each of the top 3 pins and 3 prs to the R of these, making sure there are 2 full prs for the workers. Weave wire through and work 3 rows in cloth st, then hang in the white prs over the inner pins, alternating with the yellow. Keep these in until the petal narrows, when they can be discarded.

Buttercup petals are shiny so the white threads provide the highlights. Make 5.

ASSEMBLING Twist the top of the stem wire into a small knob and cover with a piece of stem tape. Round this bind on the stamens, then the petals and calyx, using half-width stem tape and leaving the pointed ends of the sepals free to turn back.

PATTERN 18

DAISY-TYPE OPEN FLOWERS

Sylko - any desired colour
Large - 11 prs
Small - 7 prs
fine wire

green stem tape
green stem wire
double-sided sticky tape

stamens - tuft of Anchor Stranded (yellow)

Make 13 petals in cloth stitch

ASSEMBLING Make a tuft of Anchor Stranded as in the Buttercup and mount on stem wire. Follow with the petals, trim the ends and add a small piece of d/s tape before placing the calyx. Bind with stem tape and spread the sepals out neatly behind the flower.

PATTERN 17 BUTTERCUP

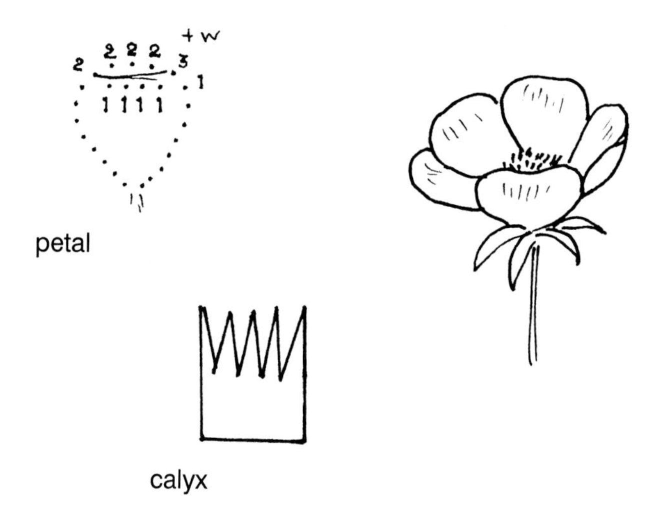

PATTERN 18 DAISY-TYPE OPEN FLOWERS

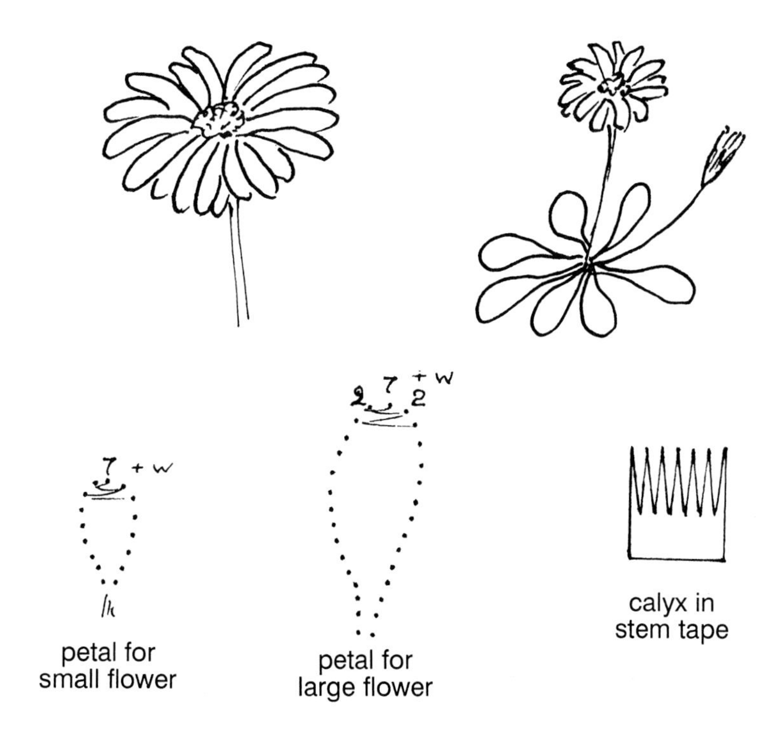

PATTERN 19

BELL-SHAPED FLOWER - Morning Glory - Convolvulus etc.

17 prs Sylko, no wire
7 pearl stamens

Make 5, 6 or 7 petals in cloth st with a single central ladder. To add deeper shading where petals join, use a darker colour for each edge passive pr.

ASSEMBLING
BUD Stitch 2, 3 or 4 petals together to form a cone, pad out with cotton-wool. Push a short hooked wire into the centre, wrap a calyx round the outside and finish with stem tape. Add dark spiralling lines in stemstitch with needle and thread.

FLOWER With the darker thread sew all the petals together from x - x to form a tube, shaping the top part with a thumb nail.
Bend over the top of a stem wire and cover with d/s tape. Tie on the stamens and thread down through the petal tube. Bind securely with self-coloured cotton. Trim the ends and tidy with d/s tape (*fig 12,* page 35 and *fig 13,* page 39). Cut out calyx shape from full-width stem tape and wrap it around the base of the flower tube. Finish off with half-width stem tape, incorporating bud stems and leaves at intervals.

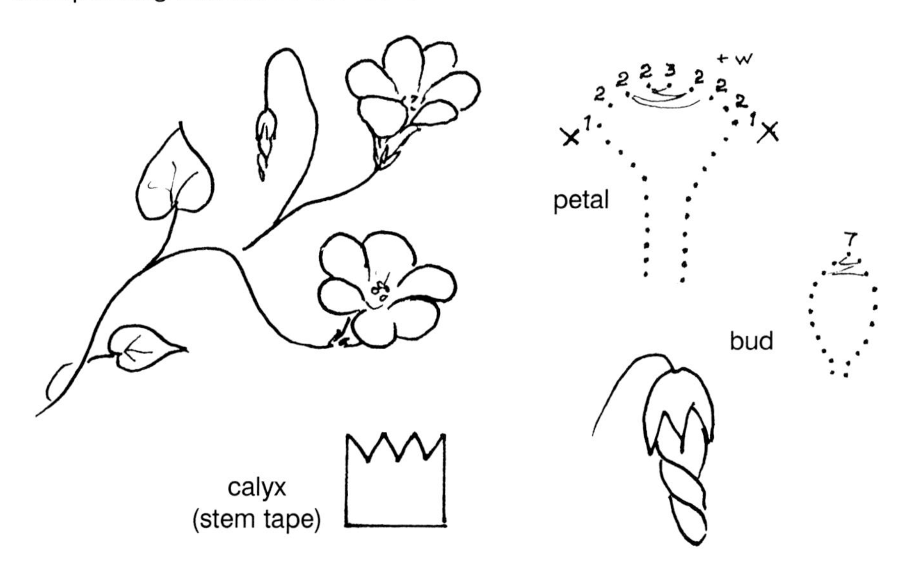

PATTERN 20

BERRIES

7 prs in shades of red and orange. Pricking on page 47
Make 3 petals in half-stitch for each (no wire).

ASSEMBLING Stitch all sides to make a ball, pushing the ends inside for padding. Cover wire with green stem tape, bend the end and push into the berry.
Sew up firmly.

PATTERN 21

HAREBELL

This is another delicate flower like the Freesia which requires finer thread. I used 7 prs Madeira Cotona 50, shade 642 mauve, with 4 prs Madeira Metallic 300 (as in the Snowdrop).

No fine wire
green stem wire
green stem tape
double-sided tape
several short stamens
3 long stamens

PETAL 11 prs no wire
Arrange the colours in prs over the top pin so that you have, from L to R, - 2 prs mauve, 1 pr metallic, 1 pr mauve, 2 prs metallic (in the centre), 1 pr mauve, 1 pr metallic, 1 pr mauve, and **2 full mauve threads** for the worker bobbins.
Twist all twice, cloth st throughout, adding one more mauve pr at the R end of row 2.
Row 4 - cloth st to centre metallic block and work a 1-twist ladder each side of this for 8 rows. Lay back prs as the petal narrows. Bow off. Make 5.

ASSEMBLING Sew petals right sides together to form a bell, leaving the 3 top holes each side free. Turn inside out, pushing just a few ends through - keeping the others to help pad out the bell.
Prepare the sepals. Mount the stamens on stem wire and pad round these with a ring of cottonwool or white stem tape to support the bell. Thread this stem through the flower tube (*fig 13,* page 39). Trim most of the loose ends on the stem very short, leaving about 6 slightly longer for security. Bind with a small piece of d/s tape and press the sepals onto this. Finish with half-width stem tape.
Assemble several flowers on a long stem. Bend the petal tips outwards and turn the ends of the sepals back. Turn the flower heads down in their natural position.

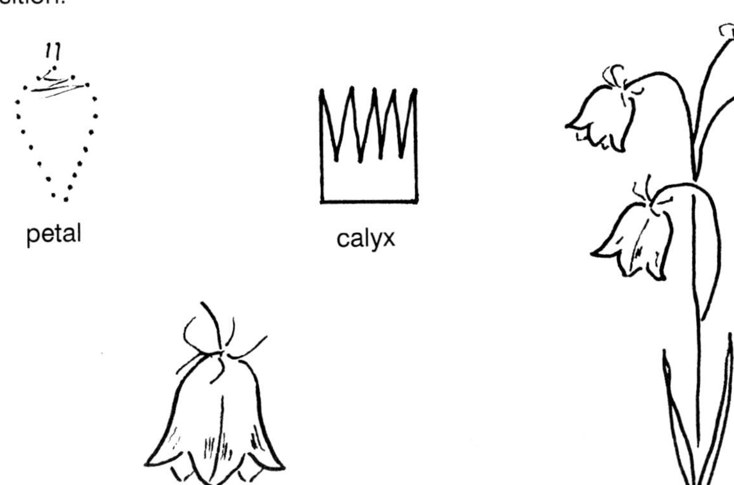

PATTERN 22

BORAGE or WOODY NIGHTSHADE (Bittersweet)

Sylko 8 prs Radiant Blue or Purple

5 small pearl stamens
5 long stamen stalks dyed purple (yellow)
fine wire
green stem tape
green stem wire
double-sided sticky tape

PETAL 8 prs plus wire
Cloth stitch. Make 5.

SEPALS cut from stem tape

ASSEMBLING Stain 5 long stamen stalks with purple felt tip pen (yellow for the Nightshade). Bind these tightly together and mount at the top of a hooked stem wire.
Place the small pearl stamens round the base of this column (*fig 18*, below) then add the petals. Trim ends, add d/s tape, followed by the sepals cut from stem tape. For the Nightshade fold the calyx round the base of the flower. For the Borage arrange the sepals so that they show between each petal when the flower is opened up.
Assemble several flowers on a longer stem, adding narrow green leaves of stem tape.

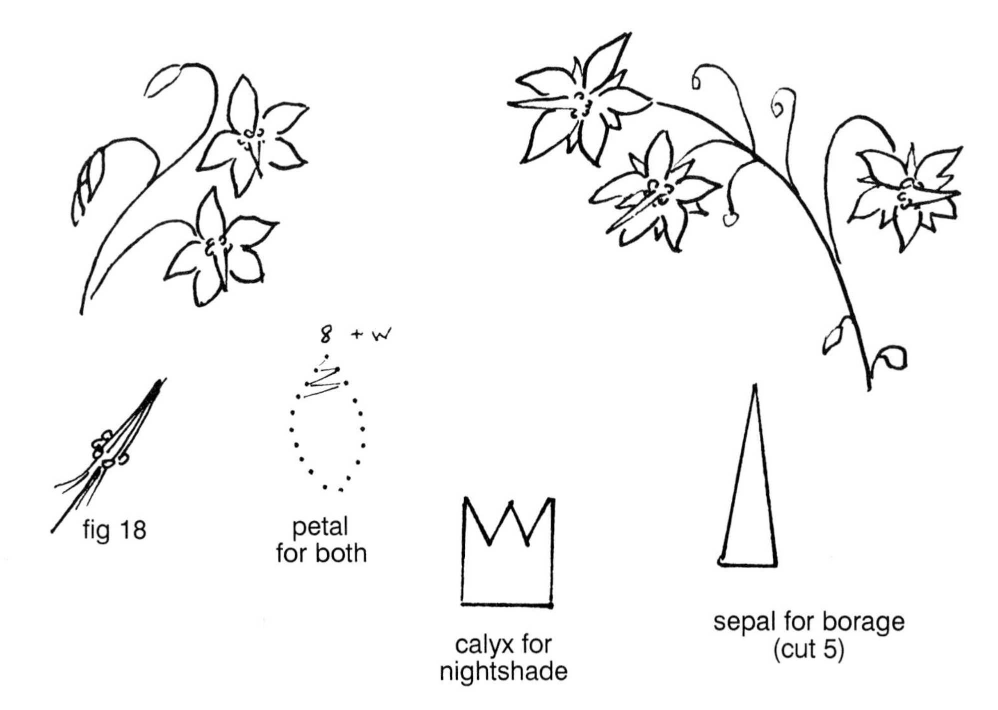

general working diagram

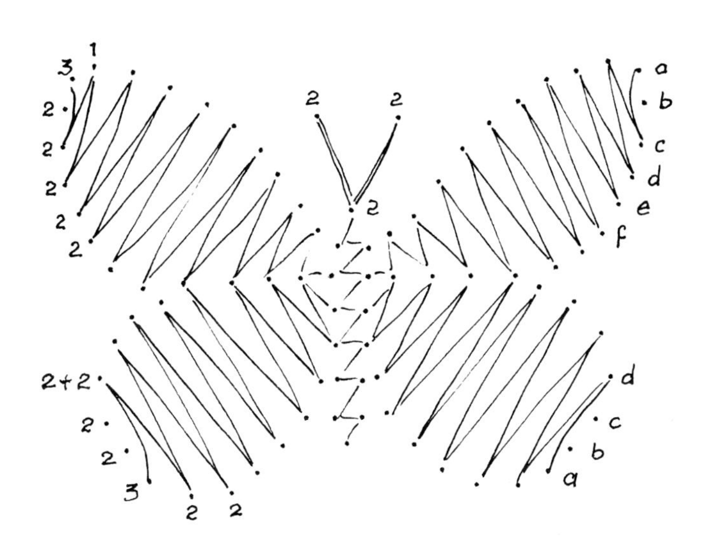

fig 19a
finishing the body

fig 19b
spot hole

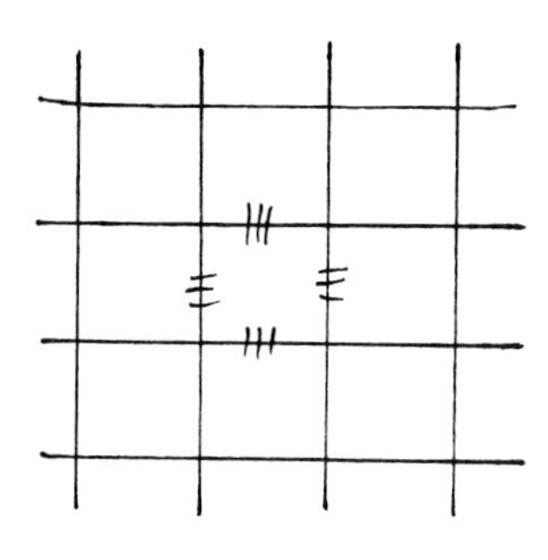

PATTERN 23

BUTTERFLIES

Although the following patterns are based on real life they are only intended as a guide to shape and size - the choice of colour can be yours, but the use of Madeira Metallic thread provides the iridescent element in the butterfly's wing.

COMMON BLUE, a small butterfly found mainly in grassland and limestone areas.

1 pr Sylko forget-me-not Blue
14 prs Madeira Metallic 40, colour 300, an iridescent white
2 prs fine lacquered wire, gauge 38

small piece of clear plastic for covering finished part of work

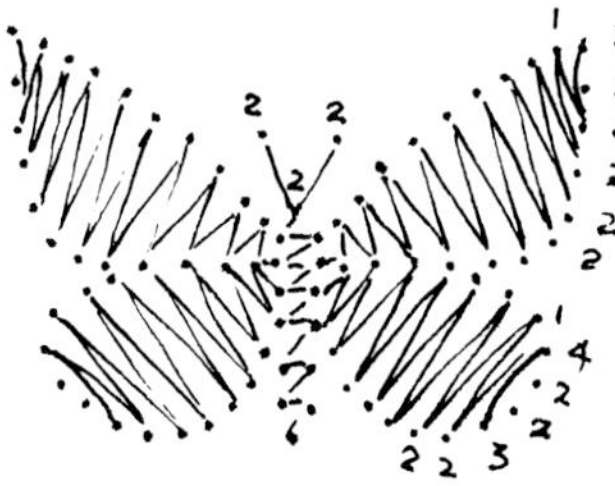

ANTENNAE and BODY
2 prs wire
4 prs Metallic white
Hang 1 pr wire and 1 pr Madeira white thread on each pin. Twist wire 3 times and pull up tight to the pin to form the club end.
Work half-st plaits to the top of the head, finishing with the white threads in the middle. Cloth st these round the pin, add 2 more white prs and use white bobbins as workers to complete the body in cloth st, keeping the twisted wire prs on the outer edges. 3 pins from the end lay back 2 white threads from the middle of the row.
Work to the bottom, bundle and bunch the remainder (B/T 8), using the wires for tying.
Lay back the bundle along the body between the pins, tie the left-out threads over this and trim neatly. Push all pins well down (*fig 19a*, page 55).
Turn pillow and adjust working cloth.

UPPER RIGHT WING 1 pr blue workers - allow about 50cm (20´´) on each bobbin of this pr.
14 prs Metallic white
1 pr fine wire

Refer to general working diagram, page 55.

Pin a - hang on 1 pr blue and 2prs white
Pins b, c -2 prs white. Twist all twice.

Weave wire through the passives (B/T 4) and tie each pr in a single knot to enclose and keep the wire up to the edge. Cloth st to R with blue worker, remove pin c, replace this between the last 2 prs and add 1 more white pr over the worker (B/T 6).

Continue in cloth st, adding 1 pr at LH pin and 2 prs at d, e, and f.
On the 4th row start single-twist ladders every 3rd stitch.
Edge st is cloth st and 2 twists round the pin.

Start laying back prs near the lower edge as the wing narrows until about 8 remain. Finish the wing, tie off the passives in pairs and lay back the wire and all but the worker and 2 passive prs. Sew these in as follows (having removed 3 of the nearest pins from the body).

Taking sewings :- Double-thread a fine long-eyed needle with one lengthened thread of the pair to be sewn in. Take this right through the nearest body hole and release the needle on the other side, leaving a big enough loop through which to push the other bobbin. When this is done gently pull up both bobbins, tie a reef knot and lay the threads to the back. Repeat this with the end passive and one in the middle. I find this method easier than with a lazy susan, especially if the needle is slightly bent near the point.

Bow off, push all the pins right down except for those on the lower edge of the top wing which are removed altogether, leaving pin-holes ready to use for the near edge of the lower wing. Trim the earlier laid back prs close to the work and all the bunched ends to about 2.5cm (1´´). Tuck these under the clear plastic or cover cloth out of the way. The metallic threads are very springy - a small piece of masking tape is handy to hold them down.

LOWER WING 1 pr blue, as upper wing
15 prs Metallic white
1 pr wire

Pin a, 1 pr blue, 2 prs white
Pins b, c, d. 2 prs white on each

Weave wire through and tie the passives (B/T 4).
Cloth st through with blue worker. Remove pin d and replace between the last 2 prs adding 2 more white prs over the worker, then 2 prs at the lower end of the next 2 rows. Introduce ladders as in Upper wing.
Complete the wing in cloth st, reducing as in the upper wing, and sewing out 3 prs into the body.

Turn pillow, cover the worked portion and tuck in the loose ends.

Work the other wings in the same way, but reading L for R and vice versa.

ASSEMBLING
Finally, bow off the bobbins, trim the earlier laid back threads close to the work and remove the pins. Gather together all the loose ends, bind and stitch into a thick stump. Trim to about 15mm (1/2´´) to form a short handle through which to stick a pin. Alternatively, the butterfly may be sewn on to a brooch pin, in which case thin out the threads and couch down the rest behind the body to form a firm foundation for the pin.

The upper wing should slightly overlap the bottom one - slip a couple of stitches through both wings near the body to hold them in place.

ORANGE TIP - common in damp meadows, woodland edges and country lanes; said to be a true sign of Spring.

1 pr Orange Sylko - this worker will be used only twice so it needs not more than 1m (1 yd) on the 'full' bobbin and 40cm (16″) on the sparse bobbin.
19 prs Madeira Metallic 40, colour 300 (iridescent white)
4 prs suitable colours for the body - I used 2 purple and 2 Madeira variegated gold
2 prs fine wire

ANTENNAE and BODY Method as Common Blue

UPPER RIGHT WING 19 prs Metallic white, 1 pr Orange, 1 pr fine wire

Hang 2 prs on each of the top 4 pins (bracketed) and 1 pr Orange for the worker.
Twist the passives twice, weave wire through, tie in single knots as in the Common Blue.
Cloth st, adding 2 prs as indicated (B/T 5) until all 19 are in.
Make **a spot hole** by twisting the workers and passives 3 times and the workers again on the following row (*fig 19b,* page 55).
In row A take the orange worker through 3 stitches, tie and lay back. Cut off the bobbins but leave enough thread to secure later with a needle.
Return to the pin, hang in a white pr and use this for the new worker to complete the wing.
Introduce 4 single-twist ladders to represent veins. Lay back prs near the lower edge as the work narrows until about 7 are left. Finish as the Common Blue.

LOWER RIGHT WING 18 prs white Metallic, 1 pr fine wire
Method as Common Blue, adding single-twist ladders for veins.
Complete butterfly as before.

ORANGE TIP

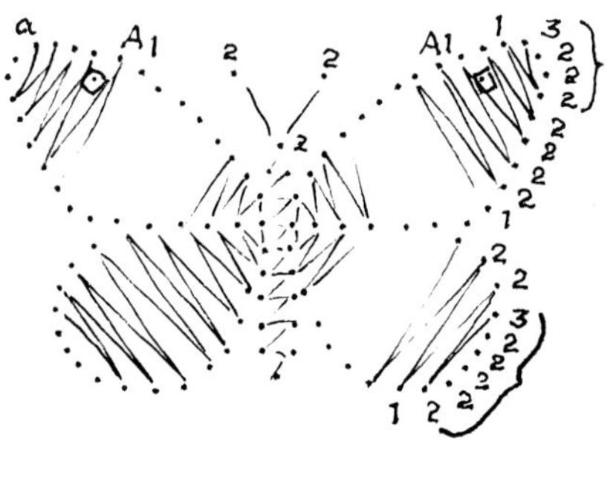

PAINTED LADY

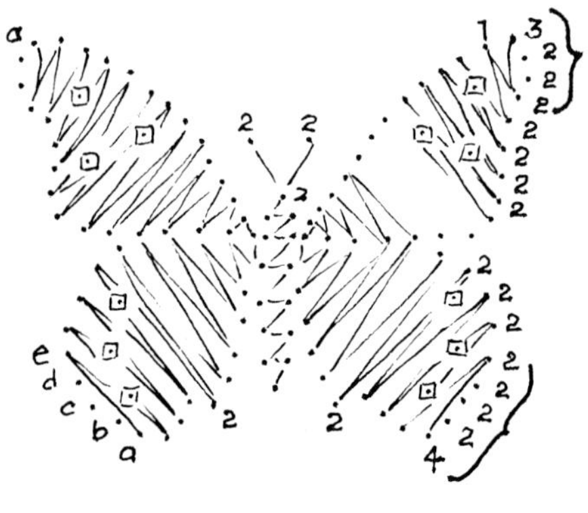

PAINTED LADY, a rapid flier and a strong migrant from North Africa
2 prs tan or orange Sylko
18 prs Madeira Metallic 40, colour Astra (variegated gold, red and petrol blue)
2 prs fine wire
small piece of clear plastic

ANTENNAE and BODY Work as Common Blue

UPPER RIGHT WING 18 prs Metallic gold, 2 prs tan Sylko, 1 pr fine wire

Pricking overleaf.
Refer to general working diagram, page 55
Pin a. - 1 pr gold, 2 prs tan (with 2 full bobbins on L)
Pins b, c, d, - 2 prs gold on each, **preferably with blue shade centrally over the pin.**
Thread wire through and cloth st through prs hanging from pins a - d.
Remove pin d and replace it between workers and wire. Tie each passive pr in a single knot to keep the wire close to the edge.
Add 1 pr gold on the next LH pin and 2 prs gold on the next 3 pins at RH edge. Keep the wire as the outside passive each side.
The wing is worked in cloth st throughout, with **spot holes** where marked - 3 twists on the worker and 3 twists on the passive each side. In the next row 3 twists on the worker again (*fig 19b,* page 55).
Start laying back prs 4 rows from the end and finally sew out the worker pr and the opposite end passive and one from the middle into a body pin-hole, as in the Common Blue.

Bundle and bunch and bow off, leaving ends about 2.5cm (1´´). Cover the wing with the plastic, tucking the ends out of the way, (secured with a small piece of masking tape).
Remove pins from the lower edge of the top wing. Turn pillow and adjust working cloth.

LOWER WING 18 prs gold, 2 prs tan, 1 pr wire

The bottom row of pin-holes for the upper wing is now used for the near edge of this wing.

Pin a - 2 prs tan, 2 prs gold
Pins b-e. - 2 prs gold on each, arranged as in the upper wing.

Weave the wire through. Cloth st from a-e with the 2 full tan bobbins and tie the passives as above. Cloth st the wing, adding 2 prs gold at subsequent pins as indicated, keeping the wire as the outside passive each side. There are now 2 prs tan, 18 prs gold and 1 pr wire in use.
Note and work the spot hole markings. Start laying back prs on the 4th row from the end, reducing to about 11. Only the workers, the opposite edge passives and a pr from the middle are sewn into the body.
Bow off and trim ends.

Turn the pillow, cover the worked portion and tuck in the loose ends.
Work the other wings and finish off as the Common Blue.

PURPLE EMPEROR - a large iridescent butterfly, elusive rather than rare, spending most of its time in the treetops.

30 prs altogether - Madeira Metallic 40, no 38, purple
Madeira Metallic 40, Astra 3, gold variegated
Sylko Bright Blue
Sylko a dark red
Sylko a dark brown (for body)
2 prs fine wire

ANTENNAE and BODY 2 prs wire and 2 prs brown. Work as Common Blue, using brown instead of white.

UPPER RIGHT WING 28 prs plus wire (19 prs Metallic Purple, including worker pr, 4 prs blue, 2 prs red, 3 prs gold, 1 pr wire)

Start with 5prs and wire on the top pin then add prs at each side, distributing the blue and red randomly. Introduce gold prs where indicated. Refer to Orange Tip instructions for the **spot holes** and working method. Remove pins from lower edge of upper wing.
Cover work with plastic, turn pillow and re-arrange working cloth.

LOWER RIGHT WING 28 prs plus wire as for Upper wing.

Make **false picots** on 10 pins along the starting edge - hang 2 prs open round each pin, mostly purple, with an extra pr on the LH pin (arrange these so that 2 **full bobbins** are at this end, placed to one side). Twist each pr 3 times, with an extra twist on the LH pr where there are different colours - this will result in separating them. Weave the wire through, tie the passives in a single knot, and using the full workers, continue the wing in cloth st, adding prs each side and forming spots where appropriate (see instructions for the Orange Tip).
Complete and assemble as Common Blue.

B4 Purple Emperor

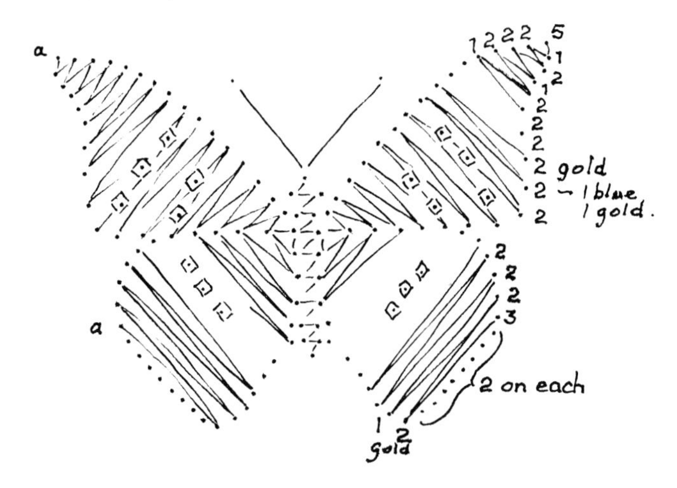

SUGGESTED THREADS

	Sylko	DMC
1. Patio rose		
Sunrise	311	754
Flame	260	947
Tangerine	113	970
Lemon	24	444
2. Rose		
Ruby	46	816
Red Salmon	234	351
Coral Pink	322	353
3. Gardenia		
White		
4. Orchids		
Pale Rose	175	819
Red Salmon	234	351
Ruby	46	816
Lemon	247	445
Old Gold	103	444
Cream	146	
Ruby	46	816
5. Carnations, Pinks		
up to 7 toning reds		
Poppy workers	525	
Pale Rose	175	819
Fiesta Pink	415	816
Red Salmon	234	351
Ruby	46	816
White		
Ruby	46	816
6. Kaffir Lily		
Gladiole Red	306	350
Orange Lily	434	351
7. Fuchsia		
Turkey Red	45	321
Ruby	46	816
Spectrum Violet	530	552
Royal Blue	8	796
8. Iris		
Wild Lilac	486	554
Ultramarine	529	552
Royal Blue	8	796
Yellow & Orange thicker thread		
9. Freesia		
Madeira Cotona 50		
DMC Broder m/c 50 variegated in		
purple 52		
yellow 108		
pinks 112		
10. Sweet Peas		
Wild Lilac	486	554
Spectrum Violet	530	553
Gütermann's 810 (good purple)		553
Light Pink	36	
Pale Rose	175	819
White		

	Sylko	DMC
11. Cyclamen		
White		
Pale Rose	175	819
Cerise	41	815
Geranium	40	602
Cerise	41	815
12. Anemones		
Reds		
Purples		
Lilac		
Heliotrope		
White		
13. Gentian		
Radiant Blue	421	995
Royal Blue	8	796
Spectrum Violet	530	553
Lime Green	297	704
14. Sparkling Snowdrop		
White		
Madeira Metallic 40, colour 300		
Moss Green	54	
Lime Green	297	704
15. Common Poppy		
Poppy	525	
Scarlet	46	666
Flame	260	947
Moss Green	54	
16. Dog Rose		
Pink and White mixed		
17. Buttercup		
Buttercup Yellow	506	
White		
18. Daisy-type open flowers		
Yellow or white		
19. Bell shapes		
Pale Rose	175	819
Ruby	46	816
20. Berries reds, yellows,orange		
21. Harebell		
Mauve Madeira Cotona 50/642		
White Madeira Metallic 40/300		
22. a) Borage or b) Nightshade		
Radiant Blue	421	
Forget-me-not	5	
b) Utramarine	529	550
LEAVES		
Light Olive	51	3347
Dark Olive	53	3345
BUTTERFLIES		
Forget-me-not	5	
Tangerine	113	970
Ruby	46	816
Radiant Blue	421	995
any brown		
Madeira Metallic 40 300 white; Astra 3 gold var; 38 purple		

BOBBIN WINDER

A cheap and efficient bobbin winder can be made by any handy DIY person, the only tool needed being a hack saw or a Getcheter ("I'll getcheter do this for me") Fortunately many of us have one of these!
A simple battery-powered fan or drink mixer provides the motor; the inside of a Gütermann spool, with a slit cut down the spindle takes the bobbin.

1. Pull the spool apart and saw a slit 5mm (1/4´´) wide in opposite sides of the spindle tube (*fig 20a and 20b* opposite).

FAN TYPE
2. Remove the fan blades and fasten the base of the spool to the top of the fan with strong glue and/or with spangle wire threaded through the holes and under each side (this makes it doubly secure).
A large spool is sometimes better than normal size, depending on the width of the fan top (*fig 20b* opposite).

3. The 2 batteries together may give too strong a spin. If this is so, take one of them out and replace it with a matching piece of wooden dowelling covered with foil to provide the contact.

4. Start winding a bobbin by hand as usual and when the thread is fast, push the spangle end down the slit tube, place the forefinger on the head, switch on and guide the thread onto the neck with thumb and 2nd finger (*fig 20d* opposite). In hot weather the blades can be replaced and the fan also used again for its original purpose!

MIXER TYPE (*fig 20c* opposite)
Remove the paddle to reveal a protruding spindle. This may fit the Gütermann spool exactly, but if not a small piece of plastic tubing or sticky tape will do the trick. There is usually only one battery in this type.

This is an invaluable piece of lacemaking equipment and I owe many thanks to my friend Vicky Radford for suggesting improvements to my original Heath Robinson idea.

BOBBIN WINDER

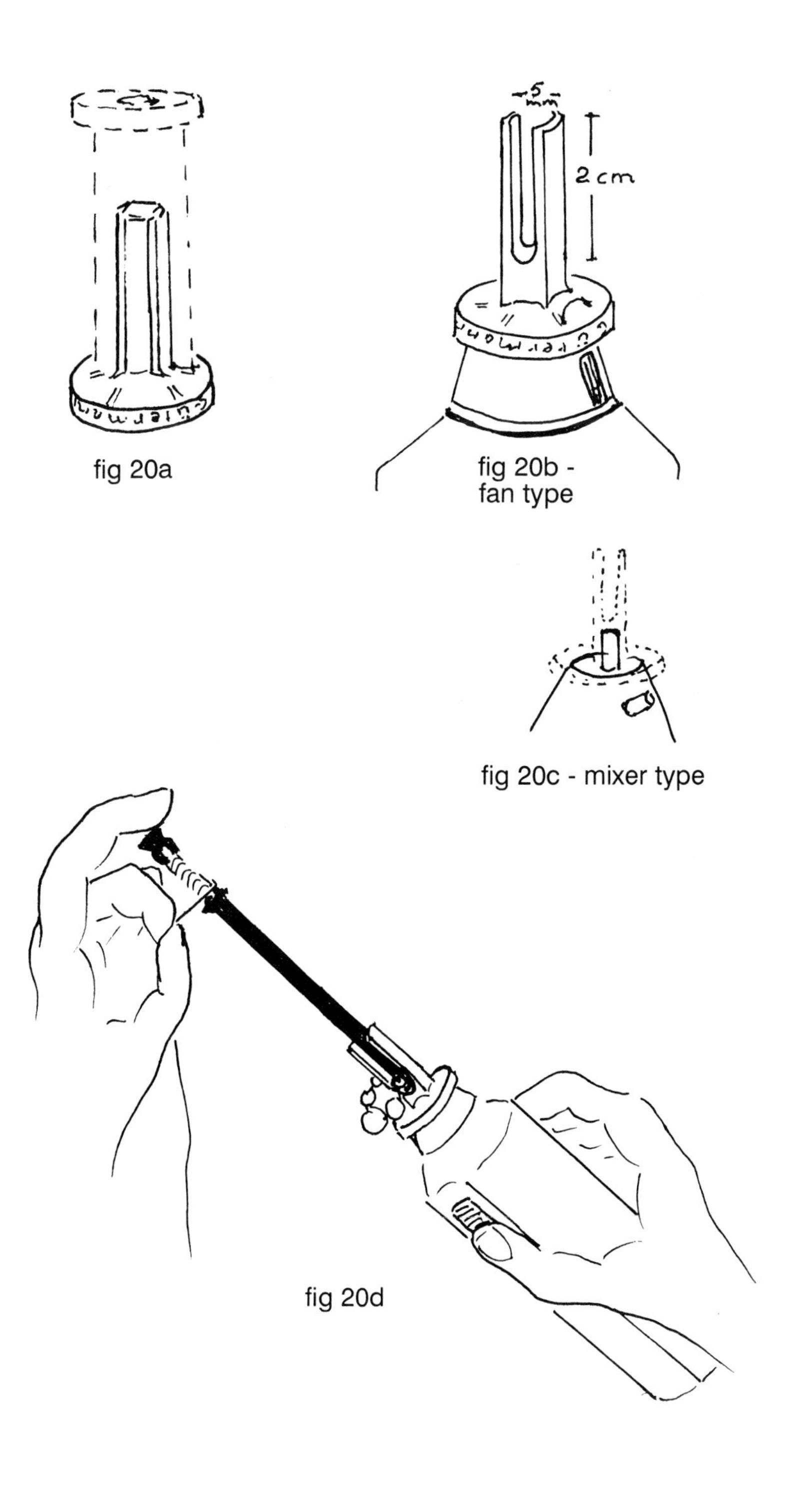

fig 20a

fig 20b - fan type

fig 20c - mixer type

fig 20d